THE JAMES NAISMITH READER

To Pete, student of the game,
fan, classmate, friend.
How could I pass by a
book on your favorite sport
edited by a man who curates
your other favorite?

Olin
December 2023

PUBLICATION SUPPORTED
WITH A SWISH GRANT
Figure Foundation

THE JAMES NAISMITH READER

Basketball in His Own Words

Edited by Douglas Stark

University of Nebraska Press
LINCOLN

The introduction previously appeared in *Wartime Basketball: The Emergence of a National Sport during World War II*, by Douglas Stark (Nebraska, 2016).

Acknowledgments for the use of copyrighted material appear on pages 245–46, which constitute an extension of the copyright page.

Library of Congress Cataloging-in-Publication Data
Names: Naismith, James, 1861–1939 author. | Stark, Douglas (Douglas Andrew), 1972– editor.
Title: The James Naismith reader: basketball in his own words / edited by Douglas Stark.
Description: Lincoln: University of Nebraska Press, 2021. | Includes bibliographical references.
Identifiers: LCCN 2020008278
ISBN 9781496219015 (paperback)
ISBN 9781496224538 (epub)
ISBN 9781496224545 (mobi)
ISBN 9781496224552 (pdf)
Subjects: LCSH: Basketball. | Basketball—History—Sources.
Classification: LCC GV885 .N185 2021 | DDC 796.323—dc23
LC record available at https://lccn.loc.gov/2020008278

Set in Questa by Mikala R. Kolander.

Frontispiece: Advertisement for the game of basketball as it appeared in *The Triangle*, January 1892. This is believed to be the first advertisement for the game since its invention in December 1891. Springfield College Archives and Special Collections.

For
Tessa Eden Stark

Contents

Preface

Minister. Inventor. Physical education instructor. Doctor.

Dr. James Naismith wore many hats during his lifetime, but the one in which he is most known for is the invention of basket ball (two words for the first few decades) in December 1891. Assigned to create an indoor game to occupy the class of "incorrigibles" during the long New England winters, Naismith harkened back to his youth in Canada to help solve this challenge that had perplexed some of his colleagues, two of whom had previously tried and failed with this particular class. In 1891 the International YMCA Training School in Springfield, Massachusetts, was a leader in teaching physical education instructors and preparing them to carry the tenets of Muscular Christianity with them as they traveled the world. Tasked by his professor Dr. Luther Gulick, Naismith created basketball, a game that has since become a global phenomenon.

Since its creation, a number of myths or misunderstandings have been perpetuated. First, James Naismith was not an American. He was a Canadian who invented the game while studying and teaching in the United States. Second, as basketball historian Chad Carlson writes, "Dr. Naismith originally created the game to be part of a college physical education curriculum. From its birth, basketball was a *college* game created by a college instructor for college students to play."[1] Third, basketball was created not with commercial interests in mind but as a form of recreation. It was designed as an activity that developed and supported good, clean living. For Naismith, this basic premise was far more important than the final score. For him, it was basketball's raison d'être.

One of the more interesting threads in the game's early development was how quickly it spread. No other sport, before or since, has caught on so quickly. The first game of basketball was held on December 21, 1891, shortly before the end of exams and the start of the holiday season. The students left campus several days later and traveled home with this new game fresh in their minds. Within weeks, basketball was being played in YMCAs and churches across the nation. Articles started to appear in newspapers in early 1892 touting this new form of winter recreation. Easy to play, it only required a form of a basket and a ball. It was not expensive. It could be played with just one or many individuals. It combined physical education with strategy. It was the perfect game at the right time. Because of this, the game quickly became popular. As Carlson points out, "Basketball also could be known as the game of missionaries. Naismith's creation traveled as far and as quickly as the YMCA students took it, catapulting from Springfield to YMCAs and colleges across the country and to Christian mission projects around the world."[2] Its rapid spread is one of the more fascinating and least understood aspects of the game's history.

Soon games were played. Leagues were formed. Players were payed. Tournaments were created. Championships contested. Rule books written and translated into multiple languages. Companies offered endorsements. The media covered the sport in print and on radio. By 1936 basketball was an Olympic sport. Not even in his wildest dreams could Naismith keep up with the game's popularity, growth, and development. It far exceeded what even he thought this game could or would become as he sat in his office in December 1891 hoping that he could find a solution to the assignment Dr. Gulick gave him. He did not want to fail the assignment. Since its invention, it seemed everyone but Naismith profited from the game. He had one endorsement, which failed miserably. He did not patent the rules. Nor did he know where the original rules were for many years. As the first coach in the University of Kansas's storied basketball history, he is the only one with a losing record. Money was raised so that he and his wife Maude could travel and witness the game's introduction as an Olympic sport in 1936. Finally, he could see firsthand how popular his invention had become. Basketball continued to snowball and snowball and not even Naismith could keep up.

One aspect of the game's creation and Naismith's role in it that has not been fully covered in the literature is what Naismith actually thought about the game. His book *Basketball: Its Origin and Development* was published 1941, two years after his death. What did Naismith think about the game? This question is one that I have thought about for many years. It led me to see what articles, speeches, letters, and correspondence I could assemble that would shed light on Naismith's views of the game. The sources compiled in this volume provide a different perspective on the game, one through the lens of Naismith. As a primary-source reader, the book is meant to promote Naismith's voice. This is an attempt to answer the question—What did Naismith think about the game?

These are his words.

Acknowledgments

Working on each book project presents its own unique challenges regarding researching and writing. Discovering what material Naismith authored about the game of basketball became a detective-type project as I tracked down material online, in repositories, and through individuals scattered in the United States and Canada. Throughout, I was able to compile a solid source of information that sheds light on how Naismith thought about the game of basketball. It is by no means complete and exhaustive, but the body of work herein is a valuable lens in understanding Naismith thoughts on the game and how it evolved during his lifetime. The journey was enjoyable and rewarding but one that required the assistance of many individuals.

Jeffrey Monseau, the college archivist at Springfield College where Naismith invented the game in December 1891, was a tremendous source of information and patience. He dutifully answered all my questions and allowed me great access to the college archive. He connected me with many individuals, including Naismith family members. Kathy Lafferty and Becky Schulte at the University of Kansas, Jayne Ptolemy at the University of Michigan, and Julien Couture at McGill University were all extremely helpful. To everyone involved, I thank you from the bottom of my heart.

Photographs for this book were generously provided by Springfield College and the University of Kansas.

Robin Deutsch for his continued work on my website, and Troy Gowen for timely scanning and other administrative functions, which always seem to elude me. A special thanks to Brenda Longstreth-Cabral for her painstaking efforts to transcribe all the original documents.

Rob Taylor, my editor at the University of Nebraska Press, was a champion of this idea from the beginning. This represents the third book that Rob and I have worked on, and each one continues to be an enjoyable experience. His insight and questions always challenge me to think differently than I originally intended. The result is always a better book. Many thanks for your support. I look forward to our next project.

As always, my family plays an important role—my parents, Marge and Alan; brothers, Jim and Nick; my sisters-in-law, Sunday and Rachel; and two nieces, Bennett and Alexis—thank you all.

Since my wife, Melanie, and I were dating, researching and writing basketball books have become a part of our lives. As we became engaged, married, bought a home, welcomed two children, and survived some health-related issues, we continued to find the time so I can work on these projects. Thanks again for your undivided love.

During the middle of this project, we welcomed our second child, Tessa Eden, into the family. We now have a strong backcourt of Ben and Tessa bringing up the ball and pressuring the opposition. It is a formidable duo. With her lean body and long fingers, Tessa looks like a future basketball player. This book is for you, my little princess, with all my love.

THE JAMES NAISMITH READER

Introduction

"Huh! Another New Game!"

As December 1891 approached, students and faculty at the International Young Men's Christian Association (YMCA) Training School in Springfield, Massachusetts, were preparing for end-of-term examinations and making arrangements to travel home for the holiday season. Another semester was coming to a close as a typical New England winter descended on the region. Most campus-wide activities were winding down. Students and faculty alike were preparing for some time away from the demands of an academic semester.

One room above the gymnasium, however, was bright with activity. James Naismith, a thirty-year-old faculty member, who the previous year was a student, was obsessed with finishing an assignment for his boss, Luther Gulick, head of the school's physical education department. The task before him was to create a new indoor game "that would be interesting, easy to learn, and easy to play in the winter and by artificial light."[1]

The assignment had formed the basis of a new course in psychology that Gulick offered for the first time in the fall of 1891. This seminar on psychology discussed a number of topics related to physical education. The class was composed of faculty members who also taught the regular student body, including the class of YMCA secretaries that was the subject of Naismith's assignment. Of particular importance was the need to find a new game that these students could engage in during the winter months. Winter sports in the 1880s were largely confined to gymnastics. The Swedish, German, and French variations of gymnastics had all been tried but more often had left the students bored and unsatisfied. The monotony of gymnastic work could not compare to the high energy of football, lacrosse, and baseball, all of which the students played with great enthusiasm the rest of the

1

year. Gulick's class began tackling the problem of finding a new game for the students to play in the winter. This particular issue engaged everyone and quickly became the central focus of the class. Midway through the semester, one class period centered on the theme of inventions, and Gulick challenged his class when he said, "There is nothing new under the sun. All so-called things are recombinations of factors of things that are now in existence."[2]

The comment piqued the interest of the students, particularly Naismith, who replied, "Doctor, if that is so, we can invent a new game that will meet our needs. All that we have to do is to take the factors of our known game and recombine them, and we will have the game we are looking for."[3] Naismith's response spurred Gulick's thinking, and he asked his students, all of whom were on the faculty—F. N. Seerley, Robert A. Clark, A. T. Halstead, Amos Alonzo Stagg, and Naismith—to each come up with an idea for a new game by the next class.

When the class reconvened the following week, however, not one new idea was forthcoming. Busy with their teaching assignments, none of the faculty members had any time to think of a new game. With the winter sports season soon approaching, Gulick realized that this problem needed to be addressed quickly so he assigned Halstead to the class of secretaries, the one class that had expressed its dislike for the current makeup of the winter sports activities. An expert in marching and calisthenics, Halstead focused on these activities with the class. After one week, he was completely discouraged by the students' response and requested a new class.

Gulick then assigned Clark to the task, hoping that he could find a more successful way to inspire the students with some form of physical activity. A gymnast by training and according to Naismith the best athlete on the faculty, Clark discarded the marching and calisthenics championed by Halstead and focused on apparatus work, his specialty. Again, the class was less than enthused. In reporting back to his colleagues the next week, he observed, "The difficulty is, with that particular group of men what we want is recreative work; something that will please them and something they will want to do."[4] Reflecting on this many years later, Naismith wrote, "Try as hard as he could, he [Clark] could arouse little enthusiasm for this kind of work."[5]

In class the following week, a despondent group of faculty members sat trying to figure out a solution. Looking again to spur discussion, Naismith said, "The trouble is not with the men but with the system we are using. The kind of work for this particular class should be of a recreative nature, something that would appeal to their play instincts."[6]

Naismith's comments challenged his colleagues, who sat quietly until Gulick broke the silence. Quickly, he turned and said, "Naismith, I want you to take that class and see what you can do with it."[7] Naismith was speechless. His comments were meant to encourage his classmates to find a solution, not to request a new assignment. Naismith was disheartened by the turn of events, and in a speech given in 1932 at Springfield College, he vividly recalled that fateful day when the responsibility of that class fell to him.

"If I ever tried to back out of anything, I did then. I did not want to do it. I had charge of a group interested in boxing, wrestling, fencing, and swimming and I was perfectly satisfied with my work. Dr. Gulick said he wanted me to do it. I had to do it or get out and I felt pretty sore about it. I thought Dr. Gulick had imposed on me by giving me something I did not want to do and compelling me to do it. As we walked down along the hall, talking about it, he said, 'Naismith, this would be a good time for you to invent that new game you said you could.' I closed my fist, and looked at Dr. Gulick's face for a spot to plant my fist, but I saw a peculiar twinkle in his eye which seemed to say, 'Put up or shut up.'"[8]

Faced with this new challenge and two weeks to solve the problem, Naismith retreated to his office above the gymnasium. He reflected back on his childhood in Canada, and the games he played as a youth.

A common misconception has developed over the years that an American invented basketball. To the contrary, Naismith was Canadian, born in Almonte, Ontario, on November 6, 1861. The second of three children, he lived with his family on Grand Calumet Island on the banks of the Ottawa River, where his father owned a sawmill. Tragedy struck in 1870 as a typhoid epidemic claimed the lives of his parents. His father died first, and three weeks later his mother passed away on his ninth birthday. Orphaned, Naismith; his sister, Annie; and their brother, Robert, moved into the home of their grandmother and their uncle Pete in a farm area between Bennies Corners and Almonte.

Growing up, Naismith was known for his strength and spent much of his time outdoors, working in the wilderness, shocking grain, and riding horses. As his grandson Stuart recalled in a 2000 interview, "One time the Mississippi River was frozen over and he thought the ice was strong enough to cross. It was not and the horse foundered and went through the ice. He worked and finally got the horse out of the water. When he was finished, he saw his Uncle Pete watching, who said, 'He got himself into that pickle and he will have to get himself out.' And he did. That was the type of childhood my grandfather had."[9]

Midway through high school, Naismith dropped out to help support his uncle and siblings. He worked for several years but eventually returned to school to complete his education. After high school Naismith enrolled at McGill University in Montreal, where he studied for the ministry. Studious about his professional pursuit, he spent all his time studying until one day a fellow classmate approached him to comment, "Naismith, we have been watching you for some time, and we see that you never take part in any of the activities. You spend too much time with your books."[10]

Soon enough Naismith was in the gymnasium, tumbling, playing soccer and lacrosse, and fencing. He also joined the football team. One day during practice the guard next to Naismith encountered a difficult situation and started swearing. Recognizing that Naismith was next to him, he stopped and said, "I beg your pardon, Jim; I forgot you were there."[11] Startled, Naismith continued practicing, but the exchange was not far from his mind. As his grandson Stuart noted, "He realized that sportsmanship was not isolated from a Godly life and decided that he was going to do both."[12] This incident, as Naismith correctly noted, changed his "career from the profession of the ministry to that of athletics."[13] It was this duality of academics and athletics, sports and clean living that eventually became the primary intellectual pursuit in his life. For the next fifty years, physical education became the central tenet of his life's work.

Naismith graduated from McGill in 1887 but elected to stay on as a physical education instructor. He began studying theology at nearby Presbyterian College, where he received his degree in 1890. Although he enjoyed studying religion, Naismith was becoming more interested in finding a way to merge physical education and Christianity, convinced that the two could coexist.

At the time the only school in North America to offer a program that trained physical education instructors was the International YMCA Training School in Springfield, Massachusetts. In the fall of 1890 Naismith traveled to Springfield to begin his studies. Upon his arrival, he met his professor, Luther Halsey Gulick, a man who would have a profound impact on his life as well as on the emerging physical education movement in this country.

Born to Congregationalist missionaries in Honolulu, Hawaii, on December 4, 1865, a few months after the conclusion of the Civil War, Luther was the fifth of seven children. For the first fifteen years of his life, he and his siblings lived in Hawaii, Spain, Italy, and Japan. His life on the move would come to characterize his own professional development and the rapidly changing fabric of the country.

After returning to the United States with his family in 1880, Gulick began his formal education. For the next two years, he was enrolled in the preparatory department at Oberlin College in Ohio. He later attended Hanover High School in Hanover, New Hampshire, and then returned to Oberlin, where he entered college to study physical education, a subject that he would have an immense influence on in the years to come. He left school a little more than a year later due to illness and eventually matriculated at the Sargent School of Physical Education in Cambridge, Massachusetts. After a brief stay there, he was again on the move and left to pursue a medical degree at the City College of New York, where he graduated in 1889.

Since he first studied physical education as a college student, the subject, though still in its infancy, had continued to fascinate him.

As a medical student, he took a job as the director of physical education of the YMCA in Jackson, Michigan. He joined the Young Men's Christian Association Training School in 1887 as head of the gymnastics department.

When Gulick arrived at Springfield, the School for Christian Workers, as it was known then, was in its second year. Prior to opening in 1885, the school had issued a statement declaring its purpose, which said in part, "There has been developed a pressing and growing demand for men qualified to enter the various fields of Christian work now open to laymen. The demand is especially pressing for men fitted to be secretaries of Young Men's Christian Associations, superintendents of Sunday-schools, and helpers of pastors in mission work and in the general work of the church."[14]

With this charge of training future YMCA secretaries, the faculty developed a course of study designed to meet this challenge. Among the courses offered were The Bible, The Outlines of Evangelical Theology, The History of Evangelical Christianity, Christian Ethics, and The Lives of Eminent Christians.[15] The YMCA became the primary vehicle for training men to uphold and pass along these values.

The YMCA was founded in England in 1844 and eventually was transplanted to the United States in the years prior to the Civil War. Its original purpose rested in providing spiritual guidance and physical help to the burgeoning group of young men who relocated to the industrial cities in the Northeast and the Midwest. After the Civil War a fundamental shift occurred in the YMCA. Rather than providing a haven for newly arrived young men, it began offering programs in physical activity such as gymnastics and calisthenics. Young men who worked in business or clerical positions joined their local YMCA and during lunch breaks or after work took classes in "physical culture." The not-so-subtle message was to encourage a more "muscular Christianity."

In the post–Civil War era American Protestants believed that society was becoming too feminine, steeped in Victorian values of humility and weakness. In its place this group of evangelical Protestants advocated a form of Christianity that viewed Jesus as an athlete and a fighter. The "strenuous life," later championed by Theodore Roosevelt, was promoted by these Christians, who believed in a new Christianity that stressed physical activity, character building, and a new manliness. The concept that sports can build a good Christian character became a central premise of Muscular Christianity.

By the 1890s the YMCA had become the foremost proponent of Muscular Christianity in America. The Progressive Era, which lasted from 1880 to 1920, witnessed one of the largest upsurges in recreation and emphasis on physical activity in the country's history. Due to the increasingly sedentary nature of work, Americans sought more physical activities. Gymnastics, bicycling, and other forms of outdoor activity became hugely popular.

With Gulick at the helm, the YMCA Training School in Springfield was at the forefront of responding to this change. Believing that a person's spiritual life develops equally from the mind and the body, Gulick invented the YMCA emblem, the inverted triangle, still in use today, that symbolizes the spiritual supported by the mental and the physical. In an article Gulick wrote about physical education at the YMCA, he made a strong case for the importance of activity to other aspects of a healthy life. "The object of our organization is to develop perfect men and we hold that the perfect man is one with his physical nature, healthy, strong, evenly developed and well disciplined; his spiritual nature strong, well balanced and trained. Either quality absent in either nature renders the individual less of a man. Each nature is an essential part of the man himself. Thus we believe that physical education is important not merely because it is necessary in order to perfect intellectual and spiritual manhood, but because the physical is in itself a part of the essential 'ego.'" He later concluded, "Our endeavor is for true symmetry, not merely symmetry of body, symmetry of mind, symmetry of soul, but symmetry of these symmetries, a symmetry of body with mind with soul."[16]

Gulick introduced sports into the YMCA, and his focus on play and activities ushered in the largest boys' sports movement the country had ever seen. His pioneering course on the psychology of play that challenged his faculty to invent new games to be played indoors reinforced this effort. The first faculty member to understand and successfully respond to this challenge was James Naismith.

With two weeks before him, Naismith set out to solve the problem of this "class of incorrigibles," as this group of YMCA secretary students was deemed by the faculty. The class was tough, and though they had already been through two instructors, Naismith certainly sympathized with them. "I felt that if I were in their place, I would probably have done all I could to get rid of the obnoxious requirements. No problems arose so long as we could get out of doors for exercise, but when Winter came, my worries began."[17] As he recalled in January 1939, "Those boys simply would not play drop the handkerchief."[18] Putting aside any reservations he may have had, Naismith forged ahead with his task.

Immediately, he laid aside the heavy gymnastic equipment and tried popular games of the era such as three deep and sailor's tag. Both games he soon discovered appealed for ten to fifteen minutes but could not sustain interest for an entire class period. He then turned to some recently introduced games including battle-ball and two games developed by Gulick, "one a modification of ante-over with a medicine ball and the other a modification of cricket."[19] These, too, proved unsuccessful.

Modifying a few of the popular outdoor games became his next course of action. He started with football and attempted to eliminate as much of the roughness as possible. He asked his students to alter the tackling style from below to above the hips. From the outset, this proved a disaster; as Naismith noted years later, "To ask these men to handle their opponents gently was to make their favorite sport a laughing stock, and they would have nothing of it."[20] Next up for Naismith was soccer. He thought that playing soccer indoors with soft-soled shoes would force the students to "use caution in kicking the ball."[21] Nothing was further from the truth, for students were accustomed to hitting the ball as hard as they could. Naismith recalled, "As a result of this, many of them went limping off the floor; instead of indoor soccer game, we had a practical lesson in first aid. I had pinned my hopes on these two games, and when they failed me, there seemed little chance of success. Each attempt was becoming more difficult."[22]

Finally, Naismith considered lacrosse, another popular game of the day and one in which he starred for the semiprofessional Montreal Shamrocks while a student at McGill. His hope was to modify the lacrosse stick, but as he wrote years later, this too was an abject failure. "In the group there were seven Canadians, and when these men put in practice some of the tricks they had been taught in the outdoor game, football and soccer appeared tame in comparison. No bones were broken in the game, but faces were scarred and hands were hacked. Those who had never played the game were unfortunate, for it was these men to whom the flying crosses did the most damage. The beginners were injured and the experts were disgusted; another game went into the discard."[23]

After trying all he could to engage the class in some form of athletic activity, Naismith was left without any answers. No new ideas. No popular game that he could modify. Nothing. Instead of trying something new, he left the students to their own devices, letting them do whatever they wanted. He stood off to the side, discouraged that none of his ideas and good intentions had worked. As the class period ended, Naismith watched as the class went to change in the locker room. He felt as if he had failed.

He later described the aftermath of that class: "With weary footsteps I mounted the flight of narrow stairs that led to my office directly over the locker room, I slumped down in my chair, my head in my hands and my elbows on the desk. I was a thoroughly disheartened and discouraged young instructor. Below me, I could hear the boys in the locker room having a good time; they were giving expression to the very spirit that I had tried so hard to evoke."[24]

Despite this discouragement, Naismith was willing to give it one more try. That night he sat at his desk and methodically analyzed each game. He thought back to the comment he had made in the seminar months earlier: "All that we have to do is to take the factors of our known games and recombine them, and we will have the game we are looking for."[25] Slowly tapping his pencil to the paper, Naismith let his mind wonder back through all the games played and tested over the past two weeks. "As I sat there at my desk, I began to study games from the philosophical side. I had been taking one game at a time and had failed to find what I was looking for. This time I would take games as a whole and study them."[26]

Using a holistic approach, Naismith soon found the answers he was looking for. First, he asked himself, what do all team sports have? He realized that all of them incorporated a ball, either a small one or a large one. Small balls used in games like baseball, lacrosse, and hockey needed some form of an implement such as a bat or stick. He thought this would be too much of an obstacle for indoor play, so instead he thought of games that used a large ball.

American rugby, the most popular game of the Gilded Age, was one that Naismith was quite familiar with. He asked himself why this game was not played indoors. The answer: it was too rough. The only way to stop a player running with the ball was to tackle him. "If he can't run with the ball, we don't have to tackle; and if we don't have to tackle, the roughness will be eliminated," Naismith mused. "I can still recall how I snapped my fingers and shouted I've got it!"[27]

Eliminating the tackling was Naismith's first big revelation. He had the outlines of the first part of the game: "In my mind, I was still sticking to the traditions of the older games, especially football. In this new game, however, the player with the ball could not advance. So far, I had a game that was played with a large light ball; the players could not run with the ball, but must pass it or bat it with the hands; and the pass could be in any direction."[28]

His final task was to create an objective. For this, he harkened back to his youth in Bennies Corners and a game, duck on a rock, that he played there. As Naismith described it, "We found a rock two feet high and two feet across. Each one took a stone about the size of his fist. One put his stone on the rock and the rest of us got behind a line and tried to knock it off. We would throw stones as hard as we could at his and if we happened to hit it, it was all right, but if we missed it, we went way down. Once in a while we threw the ball in such a way that it would knock [the other player's] off and come back again and we would walk up and get it."[29] Naismith, in remembering his childhood game, had found the answer: a game in which players tossed a ball at a vertical goal, based on accuracy and not roughness.

The next day Naismith, hoping that this new game would be the answer, entered the gym several hours before the class arrived. He carried with him a soccer ball but realized that he still needed two goals for the students to toss the ball at.

"As I walked down the hall, I met Mr. Stebbins the superintendent of buildings," Naismith wrote years later in *Basketball: Its Origin and Development*. "I asked him if he had two boxes about eighteen inches square. Stebbins thought a minute and then said: 'No, I haven't any boxes, but I'll tell you what I do have. I have two old peach baskets down in the store room, if they will do you any good.'"

Naismith took him up on the offer. "I told him to bring them up, and a few minutes later he appeared with the two baskets tucked under his arm. They were round and somewhat larger at the top than at the bottom. I found a hammer and some nails and tacked the baskets to the lower rail of the balcony, one at either end of the gym."[30]

Once the task was completed, Naismith retreated briefly to his office to write the rules. After about an hour, he came back downstairs and handed them to Mrs. Lyons, the secretary, to type up and post outside for the students. The original thirteen rules state:

1. The ball may be thrown in any direction with one or both hands.
2. The ball may be batted in any direction with one or both hands (never with a fist).
3. A player cannot run with the ball. The player must throw it from the spot on which he catches it, allowance to be made for a man who catches the ball when running if he tries to stop it.
4. The ball must be held by the hands. The arms or the body must not be used for holding it.
5. No shouldering, holding, pushing, tripping, or striking in any way the person of an opponent shall be allowed; the first

infringement of this rule by any player shall count as a foul, the second shall disqualify him until the next goal is made, or, if there was evident intent to injure the person, for the whole of the game, no substitute allowed.

6. A foul is striking at the ball with the fist, violation of Rules 3, 4, and such as described in Rule 5.

7. If either side makes three consecutive fouls it shall count as a goal for the opponents (consecutive means without the opponents in the meantime making a foul).

8. A goal shall be made when the ball is thrown or batted from the grounds into the basket and stays there, providing those defending the goal do not touch or disturb the goal. If the ball rests on the edges and the opponent moves the basket, it shall count as a goal.

9. When the ball goes out of bounds, it shall be thrown into the field of play by the person first touching it. He has a right to hold it unmolested for five seconds. In case of a dispute the umpire shall throw it straight into the field. The thrower-in is allowed five seconds; if he holds it longer it shall go to the opponent. If any side persists in delaying the game the umpire shall call a foul on that side.

10. The umpire shall be the judge of the men and shall note the fouls and notify the referee when three consecutive fouls have been made. He shall have the power to disqualify men according to Rule 5.

11. The referee shall be the judge of the ball and shall decide when the ball is in play, in bounds, to which side it belongs, and shall keep the time. He shall decide when a goal has been made and keep accounts of the goals, with any other duties that are usually performed by a referee.

12. The time shall be two fifteen-minute halves, with five minutes rest between.

13. The side making the most goals in that time shall be declared the winner. In the case of a draw the game may, by agreement of the captains, be continued until another goal is made.

Once the rules were posted and the two peach baskets affixed on the top of the balcony of the running track, Naismith took the soccer ball and went inside the gym. He nervously awaited the students' arrival and hoped that this game would finally end the trouble with this class. This was his last idea. If the class did not take to this game, he would be forced to tell Gulick that his ideas had not worked.

At eleven thirty that morning, shortly before the lunch hour, the class arrived wearing the standard gray pants and matching sweatshirts typical of physical education classes at the time. As they viewed the two baskets and read the rules, grumbles passed among the students. "Huh! Another new game!"[31] "Just try this one game," Naismith pleaded. "If you don't like it, I promise I won't try to invent another one." Without any further delays, the first game began.

"There were 18 in the class," Naismith wrote years later. "I selected two captains and had them choose sides. I placed the men on the floor. There were three forwards, three centers, and three backs on each team. I chose two of the center men to jump, then threw the ball between them. It was the start of the first basketball game and the finish of trouble with that class."[32]

The class played the entire period, and by all accounts everyone enjoyed the new activity. William R. Chase, of New Bedford, Massachusetts, made the first and only basket. The final score was 1–0.

That first game was a crude predecessor of the game as it is played today. Rough and awkward, it more resembled a game of keep away than it did basketball. Ernest Hildner was a member of that first class. In December 1966, nearly seventy-five years after that first game, Hildner gave the most complete and possibly only interview that has survived regarding that historic game. The interview, which was taped on cassette, has been stored in a box at the Naismith Memorial Basketball Hall of Fame, in Springfield, undisturbed for more than twenty years until I listened to it. Although the years may have dimmed his memory, Hildner's recollections are insight into the primitive nature of the game and a testament to the appeal generated by this new activity.

"Jimmy picked the sides, and he said there are so many people and we'll divide the class in half," Hildner recalled in the interview.

He said the object of the game is to pass the ball and get it in the other fellow's basket. We began playing basketball, and there were about fourteen fellows on each side, and the gym was so small it would not hold them all. So he threw out the ball and said go to it fellows. And that was it.

There was no time in the game. Nothing, if you could just understand how absolutely everything was gathered around how one side was shoving the ball one way and the other side was shoving the ball the other way. There were so many men that they could not operate. The gym was too small. They couldn't find a place to land.

We passed the ball back and forth. That is all there was for a while. We played this game of one side throwing the other side and the other side throwing the other side. It wasn't very pleasant.

It was just one side against the other side and smash into the other guy. The other guy would try to pass it, and he would get caught and someone would grab him. It was just a game of throwing the ball so as to get it in the other fellow's basket.[33]

One of Hildner's classmates that first day was Ray Kaighn, a Philadelphia native, who sixty-eight years after that first game, also recalled some of the details in an article in the *Philadelphia Inquirer*. "We used a soccer ball. Just as the players of today, the players then all wanted to shoot. We were all tired of Swedish calisthenics. We wanted a winter sport with the excitement of football but without its danger."[34] It appeared that they had found what they were looking for.

After the invention of basketball, Naismith and Gulick worked together for a few more years before Naismith moved to Colorado. Gulick, meanwhile, stayed at Springfield until 1903. During those years, he continued as the head of the gymnastics department, while also serving as an international secretary for the physical training department at the YMCA. He also acted as the secretary for the American Association for the Advancement of Physical Education.

When he departed Springfield in 1903, Gulick entered a period of his life that contributed greatly to his legacy, one in which he further developed his ideas of play and physical education. He moved to New York City, where he became the first director of physical education for the city public schools. He became involved in many related issues, including chairing the Physical Education Training Lecture Committee of the St. Louis Exposition in 1904 and serving as a member of the U.S. Olympic Committee for 1906 (Athens) and 1908 (London). He taught, lectured, consulted, and wrote a number of books, many of which became required reading for students of physical education and hygiene.

Gulick was a founding member of the Boy Scouts of America and, together with his wife, founded the Campfire Girls. In the later years of his life, he was quite active and founded a number of other organizations, including the American Folk Dance Society and the Playground Association. In 1918, toward the end of World War I, he served as chairman of the YMCA's International Committee on Physical Recreation of the War Work Council. In that capacity he traveled to France and interviewed servicemen about sex hygiene and their moral and physical well-being. He died later that year at the age of fifty-three.

From the moment Naismith threw up the first ball, basketball's newness earned it an expanding group of admirers. Its popularity spread so fast that within weeks the game was played in YMCAS across the country. Naismith's first game, the one he introduced to his students, is often credited with being on December 21, 1891, days before the Christmas break. Armed with this new indoor game and a growing sense of curiosity, the "eighteen incorrigibles" brought it with them to their hometown YMCAS. Writing an article in *The Rotarian* in January 1939, less than a year before his death, Naismith noted, "The prospective leaders of youth, in schools at Springfield, found this game interesting, and they took it with them as they spread their tasks as YMCA secretaries through the United States, or became missionaries in other lands."[35]

The first official game occurred in March 1892, between "the teachers of the International Young Men's Christian Association training school and the students." More than two hundred spectators watched that game. They included Naismith, Gulick, and Stagg, among others. "The teachers worked hard and performed wonders of agility and strength, but were not 'in it' with the students, who had the advantage in science, and the score at the end was 5–1 in favor of the latter."[36] The most noteworthy figure was Amos Alonzo Stagg. "The most conspicuous figure on the floor was Stagg, in the blue Yale uniform, who managed to have a hand in every scrimmage. His football training hampered him, and he was perpetually making fouls by shoving his opponents. He managed, however, to score the only goal that the instructors made."[37]

By April 1892 this new game of basketball had made its way into the *New York Times*. On April 26, 1892, the *Times* wrote a four-paragraph article under the header "A New Game of Ball: A Substitute for Football without Its Rough Features." The article notes, "The game is played with an ordinary association football, and the object of each team is to get the ball into its opponent's goal. The top of the basket is about nine feet above the ground, and a ladder is necessary to take the ball out after a goal has been made. When a player gets the ball he is not allowed to run with it, but must stand and pass it to some other member of his own team within fifteen seconds after he touches it."[38] The *Times* observed that "a match was played between the Twenty-third Street Branch of the Young Men's Christian Association and a team composed of members of the Students' Club. The students won by a score of 1 to 0."[39]

In October 1892, ten months after the game's inauspicious beginnings, a friend of Naismith's wrote, "It is doubtful whether a gymnastic game has ever spread so rapidly over the continent as has 'basketball.' It is played from New York to San Francisco and from Maine to Texas, by hundreds of teams in associations, athletic clubs and schools."[40] Indeed, the game's instant popularity has been unmatched in the history of sport.

Within a few years many colleges across the country supported basketball teams that competed against YMCAs and other college squads. Naismith's fellow instructor and friend, Amos Alonzo Stagg, left the

International YMCA Training School in 1892 to become the first athletic director at the University of Chicago. Naturally, he brought the game with him, and shortly thereafter basketball was added to the athletic schedule.

Charles O. Bemies, a student at Springfield, was captivated by the game. In 1892 he left Springfield and became the athletic director and football coach at Geneva College, in Beaver Falls, Pennsylvania. When he arrived in western Pennsylvania, so too did the game of basketball. In April 1893 Geneva played its first game against the New Brighton YMCA. In the team's only game that year, it defeated New Brighton 3–0.

In 1893, less than two years after Naismith invented the game, YMCAS across the country had formed basketball leagues. Colleges started introducing the game at roughly the same time as the YMCA. The University of Iowa began playing in 1893, and Hamline University in St. Paul, Minnesota, played its first game against the Minneapolis YMCA that same year. Played in the basement of the Science Building at Hamline with nine-foot ceilings, the local YMCA defeated Hamline 13–12. Also that year Vanderbilt University defeated a team from the Nashville YMCA 9–6. As the middle of the decade approached, the game was becoming more widespread in the collegiate ranks. On February 9, 1895, the Minneapolis State College of Agriculture defeated Hamline 9–3 in what is believed to be the first intercollegiate game.

By the end of the nineteenth century, basketball was being played in fifteen different countries. YMCA students who were sent to foreign YMCAS shared the game, helping to introduce basketball to China, Japan, and India as well as to Canada and other countries. What started as a class assignment was now a popular new game spreading to all parts of the globe.

While the game was being introduced to all parts of the globe, it was gaining popularity in the states. A mere seven years after the game was invented, a professional basketball league was founded that paid players to play the game. The National Basketball League debuted in 1898–99, and although the moniker suggests it encompassed teams nationwide, that was hardly the case. Early professional basketball had its strongest roots in the Trenton-Philadelphia corridor. Many of the early professional leagues were based in that general vicinity, and the National Basketball League of 1898–99 was no different. That first league had six teams—three based in Trenton, Millville, and Camden, New Jersey, and three in Philadelphia and Germantown. The Philadelphia Clover Wheelman, the Germantown Nationals, and the Hancock AA all dropped out, leaving the first official professional title to be contested among the three New Jersey teams. The Trenton Nationals claimed the inaugural championship, sporting an 18-2-1 record.

Despite the uncertainty of the three teams dropping out, the National Basketball League returned for its sophomore season and continued play for five seasons until the 1902–3 season concluded. In Philadelphia the Philadelphia Basketball League replaced the National Basketball League and lasted for seven seasons, from 1902–3 to 1908–9. After that the Eastern League became the most successful of the early professional basketball leagues, enjoying the longest tenure among them. From 1909–10 to 1932–33 the Eastern League became the most stable league of the game's early years.

Professional basketball, though, was not confined to the Trenton-Philadelphia corridor. Soon the game spread through New England and New York State. Leagues such as the New England Basketball League, the Western Massachusetts Basketball League, the New England Basketball Association, the Western Pennsylvania Basketball League, the Central Basketball League, the New York State League, the Pennsylvania State League, the Interstate League, the Metropolitan Basketball League, and the Connecticut State League all came and went, helping to spread the game's emerging popularity. Many of the early pioneers of the game and future members of the Naismith Memorial Basketball Hall of Fame, including Ed Watcher, Barney Sedran, and Max Friedman, all made a name for themselves in these early leagues.

It was not until 1925–26, though, that the first major attempt to create a national basketball league was made. The American Basketball League (ABL) lasted six seasons from 1925–26 to 1930–31, before the effects of the Great Depression caused the commissioner John J. O'Brien to suspend operations. Prior to that, however, the league was successful, and franchises stretched from the East Coast to Chicago. Teams were located in Philadelphia, Chicago, Rochester, Brooklyn, Washington DC, Cleveland, Detroit, Fort Wayne, and Toledo. The league made an impact, including forcing all players to sign exclusive contracts. As Robert Peterson, author of *Cages to Jump Shots: Pro Basketball's Early Years*, notes, "The advent of the American Basketball League spelled doom for the old professional basketball game because the new league adopted AAU rules almost in toto. Cages and the double dribble were outlawed in the ABL. Henceforth the professional game would gradually become faster and depend less on bulk and strength and more on speed, agility, and cleverness."[41] The league enjoyed success, including the participation of the Original Celtics, the game's first great professional team. The league, however, could not withstand the effects of the Great Depression, and after the conclusion of the 1930–31 season, it suspended operation.

When the league resumed in 1933–34, it was no longer national in scope but rather a regional league concentrated in the New York, New Jersey, and Pennsylvania area. Teams that first season were located in Trenton, Brooklyn, Philadelphia, Newark, Hoboken, and New Britain. During the 1930s the ABL was the premier professional basketball league in the country. The Philadelphia SPHAS, an all-Jewish squad, dominated league play and captured seven titles in thirteen seasons. Soon the ABL would have competition from the National Basketball League (NBL), which began as the Midwest Basketball Conference in 1935–36. By 1937–38 the NBL was poised as a strong midwestern circuit, with teams in Akron, Buffalo, Oshkosh, Fort Wayne, Indianapolis, and Dayton. The NBL eventually overtook the ABL in prestige and popularity, but until then basketball had two professional circuits as the 1930s came to a close.

At the start of the 1939–40 basketball season, the game lost its founder. On November 28, 1939, with the Thanksgiving holiday past and the 1939–40 season just under way, newspapers and radios across the country reported that James Naismith had died of a cerebral hemorrhage. He was seventy-eight years old. The *New York Times*, in its obituary, noted that more than twenty million people were now playing the game worldwide. "The fast, sprightly, colorful basketball of today, enjoyed in many lands by the young of both sexes in college, school, club, association and society gymnasiums and on professional courts, bears at least the same resemblance to the early game as that of a modern airliner to the Wright brothers' first 'flying machine'. The father of basketball had the distinction of originating the only major sport created in the United States."[42]

After inventing the game of basketball in December 1891, Naismith had continued to teach at the International YMCA Training School in Springfield until 1895. Initially, he stayed involved with the game, printing its rules, first in 1892 with *Rules for Basket Ball*. Gulick joined Naismith, and the two collaborated on printing the rules for two years before Naismith left Springfield. After he left, he had virtually no contact with the game, its development, or advancing the rules and regulations. His sole interest was in collecting foreign editions of the printed rules of the game.

Seeking to tackle another challenge in his life, Naismith, his wife, Maude, and their young family left western Massachusetts and headed for Denver, where he enrolled at Gross Medical College. While earning his medical degree, the father of basketball continued his association with the YMCA movement, serving as physical education director at the Denver YMCA. "While in Denver, he experienced a terrible tragedy," his grandson Stuart Naismith recounted. "He was spotting a young lad in gymnastics, and the child fell and broke his neck and later died. My grandfather was heartbroken. It was one of the great tragedies of his life."[43]

In 1898 Naismith joined the faculty at the University of Kansas in Lawrence as a professor of physical education and university chaplain, but he never practiced medicine. He would remain there until his death in 1939. As one would expect, Naismith became the school's first basketball coach. He compiled a 55-60 career record, the only coach in school history to have a losing record. As the game spread and grew in popularity in the ensuing decades after it was invented,

Naismith seemed to have little interest in the game. He played it twice, once in 1892 shortly after inventing it and then in 1898 after arriving at Kansas. By his own admission, he "just didn't get around to playing."[44] The two times he did play, he remembered committing a number of fouls. "I guess my early training in wrestling, boxing and football was too much for me," he later reflected. "My reflexes made me hold my opponents. Once I even used a grapevine wrestling clamp on a man who was too big for me to handle."[45]

He was humble about the recognition he received and often remarked that he did not deserve all the attention that had been bestowed on him. "You fellows have put me in a class with Abner Doubleday, who invented baseball. If basketball filled a need in the winter sports picture, I am glad, but I had nothing to do with making it grow. Honestly, I never believed that it ever would be played outside of that gymnasium in Springfield."[46]

Basketball to him was just one episode in a long series of career choices designed to improve how people lived their lives, physically and socially. His sole interest lay in counseling students. When one of his students, Forrest "Phog" Allen, told Naismith he was going to accept a job coaching basketball at Baker University, also in Kansas, Naismith quipped, "Why, you can't coach basketball, you just play it."[47] Allen later became one of the most successful coaches in college basketball history.

As Naismith's grandson Stuart recalled, "He looked upon basketball as a game to play, get physical exercise and to gain skills."[48] During his long-tenured career in Lawrence, Naismith counseled many students on life lessons and never strayed far from his Springfield teachings of "a sound mind is a sound body." John McLendon, one of his students at Kansas and later a pioneer African American Naismith Memorial Basketball Hall of Fame coach, summed up Naismith's philosophy: "Naismith believed you can do as much toward helping people become better people, teaching them the lessons of life through athletics than you can through preaching."[49] Naismith's thoughts about basketball and its relationship to physical education are evident in his writings during his lifetime.

1

Origins, Growth, and Development

Unlike other sports, basketball can trace its origins to a single individual at a certain moment in time. James Naismith was given an assignment as part of his physical education class to create a game that the students could play during the winter months. With two weeks to go before the end of the school semester and the beginning of the holiday season, Naismith tried many adaptations of existing games before developing the framework for basketball. The first game was played with nine men to a side, and the final score was 1–0. It was immediately a success and soon spread throughout the country and internationally. A month after its invention, Naismith wrote about the game for his school newspaper, *The Triangle.* Two years later, he and Luther Gulick co-authored a similar piece, published by the Spalding Athletic Library. As time went on, he gave a speech to the NCAA, wrote articles, and spoke in the early 1930s at Springfield College about the game's invention. As the years passed, he assumed more and more liberties in the telling of the story. Finally, in 1941, two years after his death, his book *Basketball: Its Origin and Development* was published, incorporating many elements from previous talks and articles. Written in clear prose, this book has since become the de facto source of Naismith's invention.

Basket Ball

The Triangle, *January 1892*

> The first article written about the game of basketball. The piece
> was authored by James Naismith and published in *The Triangle*,
> the official publication of the International YMCA Training School,
> in January 1892.

We present to our readers a new game of ball, which seems to have
those elements in it which ought to make it popular among the Associations. It fills the same place in the gymnasium that foot ball does
in the athletic field. Any number of men may play at it, and each one
get plenty of exercise; at the same time it calls for physical judgment,
and co-ordination of every muscle, and gives all-around development.
It can be played by teams from different Associations, and combines
skill with courage and agility so that the better team wins.

The ground is the gymnasium floor cleared of apparatus (it may be
shoved behind the side lines), though it could be played in the open
air, at a picnic, etc. When there is a running track around the gymnasium, the ground might be marked out just under the track, and
the baskets hung up, one at each end on the railing. All outside of this
line is then out of bounds. When there is no running track, the ends
may be cleared of apparatus, and the goals fixed on the wall, then a
line may be drawn along the sides of the gymnasium about six feet
from the walls, or enough to clear the apparatus. Across these lines
would be out of bounds.

The goals are a couple of baskets or boxes about fifteen inches in
diameter across the opening, and about fifteen inches deep. These
are to be suspended, one at each end of the grounds, about ten feet
from the floor. The object of the game is to put the ball into your
opponents' goal. This may be done by throwing the ball from any

part of the grounds, with one or both hands, under the following conditions and rules:—

The ball to be an ordinary *Association* foot ball.

1. The ball may be thrown in any direction with one or both hands.
2. The ball may be batted in any direction with one or both hands (never with the fist).
3. A player cannot run with the ball. The player must throw it from the spot on which he catches it, allowance to be made for a man who catches the ball when running at a good speed if he tries to stop.
4. The ball must be held in or between the hands, the arms or body must not be used for holding it.
5. No shouldering, holding, pushing, tripping, or striking in any way the person of an opponent shall be allowed; the first infringement of this rule by any player shall count as a foul, the second shall disqualify him until the next goal is made, or, if there was evident intent to injure the person, for the whole of the game, no substitute allowed.
6. A foul is striking at the ball with the fist, violation of rules 3, 4, and such as described in rule 5.
7. If either side makes three consecutive fouls, it shall count as a goal for the opponents (consecutive means without the opponents in the mean time making a foul).
8. A goal shall be made when the ball is thrown or batted from the grounds into the basket and stays there, providing those defending the goal do not touch or disturb the goal. If the ball rests on the edges, and the opponent moves the basket, it shall count as a goal.
9. When the ball goes out of bounds, it shall be thrown into the field of play by the person first touching it. In case of a dispute, the umpire shall throw it straight into the field. The thrower in is allowed five seconds, if he holds it longer, it shall

go to the opponent. If any side persists in delaying the game, the umpire shall call the foul on that side.

10. The umpire shall be judge of the men and shall note the fouls and notify the referee when three consecutive fouls have been made. He shall hive power to disqualify men according to Rule 5.

11. The referee shall be judge of the ball and shall decide when the ball is in play, in bounds, to which side it belongs, and shall keep the time. He shall decide when a goal has been made, and keep account of the goals with any other duties that are usually performed by a referee.

12. The time shall be two fifteen minutes, halves, with five minutes' rest between.

13. The side making the most goals in that time shall be declared the winner. In case of a draw, the game may, by agreement of the captains, be continued until another goal is made.

This game is interesting to spectators as well as to the players, and may be made quite scientific by good judgment combined with good co-ordination. Several good points have been scored by two or three players working together. The number composing a team depends largely on the size of the floor space, but it may range from three on a side to forty. The fewer players down to three, the more scientific it may be made, but the more players the more fun, and the more exercise for quick judgment.

The men may be arranged according to the idea of the captain, but it has been found advantageous to have a goal keeper, two guards, three center men, two wings, and a home man stationed in the above order from the goal.

It shall be the duty of the goal keeper and the two guards to prevent the opponents from scoring. The duty of the wing man and the home man is to put the ball into the opponents' goal, and the center men shall feed the ball forward to the man who has the best opportunity, thus nine men make the best number for a team.

It is well suited for boys. Director Finch has introduced it in his boys' classes with apparent success. We wish that the physical directors would try the game, and report any points that might be amended.

It is intended that this game should be free from much of the reputed roughness of Rugby, and in the framing of rules this has been kept strictly in view. If some of the rules seem unnecessarily severe, it will be remembered that the time to stop roughness is before it begins.

A gymnasium is bounded by hard walls, and has a pretty solid floor and for that reason, any shoving that would injure a person must be stopped. *e.g.*, when a man raises his arms to throw the ball, another might give him the shoulder, and disable him, but if this is stopped there will be an understanding that it is not allowed. It is for the benefit of a physical director that no man be hurt in his gymnasium, so that any director who tries it should make every man conform to the rules strictly at first, and then he would soon get accustomed to playing ball instead of trying to injure his neighbor, when it is nothing but a friendly tussle in which they are taking part.

The very men who are rough in playing will be the very first ones to oppose the game on the account, for there is that in man's nature which will retaliate, and the rough player generally gets the worst of the roughness. If there is need for such a game, let it be played as any other game of science and skill, then men will value it. But there is neither science nor skill in taking a man unawares, and shoving him, or catching his arm and pulling him away, when he is about to catch the ball. A dog could do as much as that.

There seemed to be no way of compensating the opponents for a foul made. Free throw was thought of, but, after a little practice, a good thrower could convert it into a goal almost every time, because of the limits of the ordinary gymnasium. Then the idea was that three fouls would count as a goal, and would be a deterrent to the making of them. This is true, for when a team finds that another foul would count a goal against them, the extra foul is hardly ever made, showing that it is possible to play the game without making fouls.

If men will not be gentlemanly in their play, it is our place to encourage games that may be played by gentlemen in a manly way, and show them that science is superior to brute force with a disregard for the feelings of others. The umpire will thus be responsible for much of the roughness if he lets it go unchecked, but if he is firm and impartial in his ruling he will gain the respect even of those who suffer at the time.

We would advise the director to keep a good firm grasp on the ruling for a while at first.

Jas. Naismith.

Basket Ball for 1894

This book, *Basket Ball*, was written by James Naismith and Luther Gulick in 1894. It was published by the Spalding Athletic Library. The book's title page lists Naismith and Gulick as instructors at the YMCA Training School in Springfield, Massachusetts, and Naismith as the "Inventor of Basket Ball."

"Basket Ball," the rules of which were first published in *Physical Education* as an experiment two years ago, has proved its right to a place among our games and has been more popular than was anticipated. It has spread from Springfield to Paris, France, in one direction, and to Melbourne, Australia, in the other. It has been found peculiarly adapted to business and professional men, as it is interesting and may be played by men of any size and in any condition of training. It has also been found valuable for girls and women, as there are few games which they can play that are not a strain on the nervous system rather than on the bodily functions. It is peculiarly adapted for giving health without involving a severe mental strain.

It has survived the various tests that have been applied to it, which instead of killing has developed it, until today there is need for a new edition of the rules with a good many amendments. In playing the game, new features have come up and as far as possible, these have been considered in the present edition. When a point comes up which is not covered by the rules, the spirit of the game must be taken into consideration, it being taken for granted that every man plays according to this spirit and not merely to avoid the eye of the umpire and referee. When either of these officials has had occasion to rule outside the letter of the law, he has been guided by the thought that was shown in making the laws.

Team play is certainly one of the strong points in the game, but this does not mean doing those things which the *letter* of the law will not cover, but does consist of perfected play between the members of the team.

There will always be more or less of diversity in the game, especially as to the size of the grounds, position of goals, kind of goals, and many other circumstances, but so long as the main features are kept clearly before the players, these minor matters will make little difference in the game. Every gymnasium has its own peculiarities, and it is only fair that any advantage of position or other detail should be given to the visiting team, unless, of course, when the game is played on neutral grounds.

Basket Ball is not a game intended merely for amusement, but is the attempted solution of a problem which has been pressing on physical educators. Most of the games which are played out of doors are unsuitable for indoors, and consequently whenever the season closes, the game, together with all the benefits to be derived therefrom, is dropped. It is true that some players have been accustomed to keep up a desultory kind of training but it lacked the all-round development that is so requisite, and very frequently failed to give the exercise for the heart and lungs which is so desirable. A number of gymnasiums have running tracks, but even then it is more or less uninteresting to run around a gallery so many times per day.

There are certain definite conditions to be met by the game, and these had to be complied with before it could be pronounced satisfactory.

1. It should be such as could be played on any kind of ground—in a gymnasium, a large room, a small lot, a large field, whether these had uneven or smooth surface, so that no special preparation would be necessary. This is especially necessary in large cities where in order to get a good sized field you must go to a considerable distance, thus rendering it inaccessible to many of the members. Basket Ball may be played on any grounds and on any kind of a surface. It has

been played in a gymnasium 12x20 and can be played on an ordinary foot ball field.

2. It should be such as could be played by a large number of men at once. This has been fully met, as the only limit to the number of men that can play is the space at command. If a great number of men wish to play at once, two balls may be used at the same time, and thus the fun is augmented, though some of the science may be lost. The men, however, are required to keep their positions a little more carefully. As many as fifty on a side have been accommodated.

3. It should exercise a man all-round: every part of his body should get a share of attention. His legs are used to sustain his body and his arms are exercised in handling an object, which is a normal function. In the bending and twistings of the trunk and limbs the vital organs receive such exercise as will make them healthy and strong. Thus in a manner, it serves the same purpose as the sum total of the apparatus in a gymnasium, while the main development is in strict accord with the idea of unity in man. It should cultivate the different energies of which he is capable. Agility is one of the prime requisites in a game where the ball must be secured before an opponent can reach it, and when obtained he must be baffled in his attempt to take it away. This also gives us grace as the perfection of action. Physical judgment is required and cultivated in handling the ball, receiving it from one of your own side, and eluding an opponent. This requires that a man should keep complete control of himself or his play is more likely to count for nothing. A wrong pass may give the opponent a decided advantage and an instant's hesitation is sufficient to lose the best opportunity that might be offered. There should also be developed that manly courage which is so essential in every true gentleman.

4. It should be so attractive that men would desire to play it for its own sake. This is one of the chief points in this game. The thorough abandonment of every thought but that of true sport

makes it entirely recreative, while the laughable side of the game may be appreciated by both players and spectators. It is made more attractive by the fact that it is a game into which competition may enter and opposing teams may try their skill, thus giving zest to those who have become proficient in the game.

5. It should have little or none of the reputed roughness of Rugby or Association football. For this reason, kicking at the ball and striking at it with the fist were prohibited. All running with the ball was done away with because when a man runs with the ball we necessarily have tackling to stop him, and it is at this point that the roughness of Rugby is most severely felt. This regulation has been criticised especially by Rugby men, but the above reasons should appeal to every one who is seeking a game which can be played without roughness. A man's whole attention is thus centered on the ball and not on the person of an opponent, and thus opportunity for personal spite is taken away. If some of the rules seem unnecessarily severe it should be remembered that the best time to stop roughness is before it begins. A gymnasium is bounded by walls, so that a push which would result in no harm on the soft turf may send a player against the wall with force enough to injure him. If the rules are strictly enforced at first the men will soon get accustomed to playing ball instead of trying to injure those who are opposed to them only for the time being, and they will soon realize that it is nothing but a friendly game. The very men who wish to play roughly will be the first to condemn the game if roughness is allowed, for it is generally they who get the worst of the roughness in the end.

6. It should be easy to learn. Lacrosse, which is considered one of the best all-round games, has this objection, that it requires too much practice in order to obtain even the exercise from the game, whereas any one can learn to play Basket Ball at a single lesson, and at the same time obtain the exercise which an experienced player gets.

These were felt to be the conditions that would determine the usefulness of a game that might be played summer and winter, in any climate, and under varying conditions.

To play a game, divide the men into two teams, hang a basket at each end of the room, let each side defend one of these goals while endeavoring to put the ball into that of their opponents'. This is done by placing the men, passing the ball from one to another and trying to throw it into the goal.

The object of a player should be whenever his own side has possession of the ball to gain an uncovered position so that his own side may pass it to him. On the other hand, his opponent should see that he does not gain this favorable position. It is at this point that head work and the ability to do a certain thing without letting his opponent know what he is about to do are valuable. Individual play does not count for much, for very often a man has to sacrifice his own *chance* of making a goal that he may be *sure* of it from the hands of another. In the gymnasium, the ball as a rule should not be passed swiftly in a straight line, but should be tossed lightly so that the one who receives it shall lose no time in passing it to another or throwing it for a goal. But on the field, where long passes may be made, the straight throw may be used to advantage.

Of course, any number of men can play when sport is the object and very often the more men the more fun, but when a match game is to be played it is necessary to have a definite number of men on the floor; for a small gymnasium, five men make the best sized team, while for a large gymnasium nine men may be put on the floor. (See rule 21). When the team consists of five men they may be placed thus: right and left backs, right and left forwards, and center.

For nine men, they are a goal keeper; two backs to assist him; a center; a right and left center; two forwards and a home man.

These are arranged in this order from the goal which they are defending. A man does not need to keep strictly to his place, but should be always in his own part of the grounds. It should be the duty of the home man and the two forwards to get a favorable position to throw for goal and to assist one another in this matter. These ought to be men who are not afraid to sacrifice their own glory for the good of the team, while, at the same time they should be cool headed enough to use every opportunity of trying for goal. The center men are placed so that they may assist the forwards or help the backs, and as the strain comes on each of these, they should be able to make a good shot for the goal and quick enough to stop a good play of an opponent. The aim should be constantly to feed the ball forward to their own men and keep them in a position to make goals. The duty of the backs is principally to prevent the opponents throwing for goal, by preventing them from getting the ball, and by taking it from them when they are preparing to throw. In this, if anywhere, prevention is better than cure, for when a ball is thrown up so as to alight in the basket there is no goal keeper who can keep it from entering. The goal keeper's duty is to get the ball away from the vicinity of his goal and to stop as many plays as possible, thus he will bat the ball more frequently than is advisable in the case of the other players.

When fun and recreation are desired, as many men as please may play, and they may be distributed according to the captain's own idea, but the best plan seems to be to divide the men into three classes, forwards occupying the third of the ground nearest the opponents' goal; center men occupying the middle third; backs occupying the defensive third of the ground. This is not a hard and fast division, but merely to let the men know for what part of the field they are responsible. The men ought to be taught to fill every position as it is intended to be an all-round game, and though each position entails plenty of hard work, yet each man is better if he be able to take any part.

THE GROUNDS

These are the gymnasium floor cleared of apparatus, though any building of this nature would suit. If there is a gallery or running track around the building the baskets may be hung up on this, one at each end, and the bounds marked out on the floor just beneath this gallery. The apparatus may be stored away behind this line and thus be out of the field of play. If there is no gallery, the baskets may be hung on the wall, one at each end. In an open field a couple of posts may be set up with baskets on top, and set at the most convenient distance. Out of doors, with plenty of room, the fields may be 150 feet long, the goal-lines running through the baskets perpendicular to the length of the field; the side boundaries 100 feet apart, the ball must be passed into the field when outside these lines. A player cannot run after he has picked up the ball, though he may throw it and endeavor to get it again, but he must throw it higher than his head; by this means he may make progress from one part of the field to another, but his opponent always has an opportunity of gaining the ball without tackling him. Again, he may bound in front of him as he runs, or dribble it with his hand along the ground, but he cannot kick it with his feet, not even to dribble it. At a picnic the baskets may be hung on a couple of trees and the game carried on as usual.

The goals are a couple of baskets fifteen inches in diameter across the opening and about fifteen inches deep. If the field of play is large the baskets may be larger, so as to allow of more goals being made. When the field is 150 feet long the baskets may be thirty inches in diameter. These are to be suspended, one at each end of the grounds, about ten feet from the floor. A neat device for a goal has been arranged by A. G. Spalding & Bros., by which the ball is held and may be thrown out by pulling a string.

The object of the game is to put the ball into your opponents' goal. This may be done by throwing the ball from any part of the grounds, with one or both hands under the conditions and rules described.

PLAYS

Side throw. This throw is made with the arm nearly straight. It is a low hard drive, hard to catch unless there is ample time and the ball comes straight. Additional impetus is given to the ball by a twist at the waist. This throw is useful in making a long, low pass across the field.

Over-hand throw. One great difficulty with the side throw is that there is usually an opponent by who will stop it. It is usually best then to throw high enough to clear him. If he is at all near, this will have to be done by this, the over-hand throw. This is an excellent method of throwing for goal.

Under-hand throw. Useful in throwing under an opponent who expects a high throw and is jumping for it. This should be made with speed.

In bringing the ball in from out of bounds there will almost invariably be a man already to stop the throw, a very common and used play here is illustrated in this cut. Feint to throw over, then throw either directly under or to one side of him. *Do not look at the ball nor where you intend to throw.* It will give the play away. The play will of course have to be made very fast.

Foul—hugging the ball. This is one of the most frequent fouls that is made in playing. The man who has the ball naturally wishes to keep it, or at least, to throw it himself. To avoid having it taken away he "hugs" it. This is a foul.

To get out of this position, he should have jerked the ball up or down, or, preferably to either, he should have given a quick turn so as to face the other direction and thus to bring his opponent at his back.

Foul—holding. At the moment of throwing, the opponent comes from behind and for an instant only throws his arms around the thrower, thus effectually spoiling a good throw.

This is particularly a foul of green players.

Foul—holding. In making a throw for goal a common method is "put" it just as a shot is "put." The opponent grasps the wrist for a moment and stops the throw. This is always a foul and counts against the side making it. If the thrower had held his left arm in front of his body so as to ward off the attack it would have been impossible.

Getting the ball. When the ball goes out of bounds, or even when it has to be picked up on the field, an opponent who is directly behind can put his shoulder up against the man's thigh, grasp the ball and pull. He will either let go or fall on his head.

Supporting each other. The secret of Basket Ball is in team play. Every time the ball is in your hands your side should free themselves from their opponents so that you can have a chance to get the ball safely to the man you have in mind. There is no game in which individual play will do less and team play more than in Basket Ball.

THROWING FOR GOAL

Some teams are throwing for goal all the time. They think, apparently, that out of so many chances some will be made. Of course this is possible and sometimes a goal will be made from the whole length of the field. This, however, is so rare as to make the side that tries it lose steadily.

Only throw for goal when there is a reasonable chance for making it. If you are so attacked that you cannot make a good throw, instead of throwing wild, pass to the other *forward* or even to the center. This is team play.

A most common fault of green players is to be continually running after the ball.

When the opponents have the ball, *stick to your man* like glue. Cover him so effectually that the ball cannot by any manner of means be passed into his hands. Follow him anywhere; prevent *his* getting the ball. When the ball is thrown then try and get it yourself if it comes your way. If instead of playing this way, you run off to block the man who has the ball, while you may make it harder for him to make a good throw, still you have left your man uncovered and the ball can and probably will be thrown to him.

Now, however, when it is one of your men who has the ball, your play must be exactly reversed. Get in front of or away from your opponent so that the ball may be thrown to you with safety.

When it is your immediate opponent who has the ball do not let him have a good throw, take the ball away from him, block him, hit the ball with your *open* hand. If you hit it with your fist it is a foul.

QUALITIES DEMANDED IN A SUCCESSFUL TEAM

1. *Coolness.*—The individual member of the team must never get rattled and play wild, perhaps in quality is more essential than this one.

2. *Quickness.*—Basket Ball is a fast game, the slow man is "not in it" at all. The man who can work fast will, other things being equal, make the best man every time.

3. *Accuracy.*—Wild throwing is one of the most frequent causes of defeat. Good throwing is not merely necessary in throwing for goal but in all the passing that is done. A wild or careless throw will give the ball to the opponents almost every time. Accuracy in throwing for goal is an absolute necessity.

   I have seen a team by fine play get the ball and work it up steadily to the forwards again and again, but the forwards were poor throwers and could not make the goal. On the other side while the ball got to the forwards but seldom, still almost every time that it did, a goal was the result. The result of this was that the inferior team won. There was one weak spot and the game was lost on account of it.

4. *Good Judgment* is a necessity. The plays must vary constantly. The tactics that will be the most effective against the team will fail against another.

   Nothing but careful watching and good judgment will enable the team to know what plays will succeed best.

5. *Endurance.*—Few games demand more endurance than Basket Ball. The running, jumping, turning, twisting, are incessant. Good heart and lungs are involved.

6. *Self-Control.*—Bad temper will often lose games. The play is so fast, the Interest so Intense, that it is all but inevitable that some fouls shall be made and it will often appear that these are intentional when they are not. Then, too, the officers cannot see everything, and the tendency will be to think that they are willfully shutting their eyes. The only way to do is to play fair yourself *under all conditions*, even if you think that your opponents are not doing so, and furthermore always take it for granted that the officers are doing their full duty. Stand up for them. Their positions are hard ones to fill. It is impossible to please everyone. The whole success of the game depends on the efficiency of the officers, and this depends usually on the support that is given them.

BASKET BALL RULES.

Copyrighted. 1893.

1. The ball is put in play as follows: The teams line up in their respective positions and the referee throws the ball up in the middle of the field. This is done at the beginning of the game, at the beginning of the second half, after each goal, when a foul has been made and whenever time has been called.

2. The ball may be thrown in any direction with one or both hands.

3. The ball may be batted in any direction with the open hand or hands.

4. The ball cannot be struck with the fists or kicked.

5. A player cannot run with the ball either in or out of bounds except as specified in rule 2. He must throw it from the spot on which he catches it, allowance to be made for a man who catches the ball while he is running, if he tries to stop. (This does not exclude turning around on the spot.)

6. The ball must be held by the hands; the arms, legs or body must not be used for holding it.

7. When the ball is passed from the field of play out of bounds in order to claim exemption from interference, or when it is passed between players, outside of bounds, the ball shall be given to the opponents.

8. When the ball is held by more than two men for any length of time, the referee shall blow the whistle and throw the ball straight up from the spot where it was held.

9. No shouldering, holding, pushing, tripping or striking shall be allowed. The first infringement of this rule shall count a foul, the second shall disqualify him but a substitute may take his place.

10. The ball is not out of bounds until it crosses the line.

11. When the ball goes out of bounds, it shall be returned by the side first holding it. The thrower in shall walk as directly towards the line as the apparatus, etc. will admit. He may then (1) bound it in and catch it, (2) throw it to someone in the field,

or (3) roll it along the ground. He is allowed five seconds to hold it and if he holds it longer than that, it goes to the opponents. In case of doubt in the mind of the referee as to which side first held the ball, he shall throw it up in the field of play.

12. A foul is violation of rules 4, 5, 6, 9, 16 and 19.

13. A goal shall be made when a ball is thrown or batted from the ground into the basket (directly or by a rebound from the sides) provided it stays in. If the ball rests on the edge of the basket and an opponent moves the basket, it shall count as a goal.

14. The score shall be counted by points. A goal shall count 3 points, a foul 1 point for the opponents. A majority of points shall decide the game.

15. The goals must be protected against the interference from the spectators, this protection to extend at least six feet on each side of the goal, and in case of a screen or other contrivance, to be at least six feet high. In case of doubt *in the mind of the referee or umpire* arising from the presence of the spectators, the visiting team shall have the benefit of the doubt.

16. Any persistent intentional delay of the game should be counted as a foul against the team so delaying.

17. The time shall be two halves of twenty minutes each or such time as the captains may mutually agree upon. This is time of actual play.

18. The referee shall be judge of the ball and decide when the ball is in play, to which side it belongs; shall keep the time, decide when a goal has been made; keep account of the goals and fouls made and any other duties not discharged by the umpire.

19. The umpire shall be judge of the men, shall note the fouls made, report to the referee, keep an account of them, and notify the offenders. He shall have power to disqualify a player according to rule 9. In case any player is needlessly rough in his efforts to get the ball, the umpire shall warn him, even though he does not make a foul, and if he persists, the umpire shall call a foul upon him or even disqualify him if he thinks it necessary.

20. Any player has a right to get the ball at any time while it is in the field of play, provided only that he handles the *ball* and not the opponent.
21. The team shall consist of five men when the actual playing space is less than 1200 square feet, and nine men when it is more than this and less than 3600 square feet.

The position of umpire is a very responsible one and on his ruling depends, to a great degree, the value of the game. If he deliberately overlooks violation of the rules he is responsible for a great deal of unnecessary roughness and consequent ill feeling, but if he is firm and impartial in his decision he will soon win the respect of all, even those who suffered at the time.

A player may stand in front of the thrower and obstruct he ball, but he must not violate rule 9. One aim of the rules has been to eliminate rough play, and for this reason the umpire must interpret with this aim in view.

It is difficult for an umpire to see what every man is doing in every play, but if he watches where the ball is going to alight he may note the few men who are actually engaged in the play and may detect fouls. He does not need to watch the ball but the men. This will simplify the work of the umpire which is difficult at best.

History of Basketball

Young Men's Era, *April 16, 1896*

> An article titled "History of Basketball," written by James Naismith, appeared in *Young Men's Era* in the April 16, 1896, edition. This was authored by Naismith while a medical student in Denver, Colorado.

In the fall of 1891, shortly after the introduction of Swedish gymnastics into the schools in some of the large cities of the east, the question arose whether this system filled the place of school gymnastics. The main objection that was brought against them was that it gave no scope for recreation, and, instead of being a rest to the mind, was a drain upon the nervous system. This was especially noticeable when, instead of being used for the purpose of education, Swedish educational gymnastics was substituted for the old fashioned recess. The main objection to this form of the work was that it required a direct control of the will. Thus the person who was practicing gymnastics was under more or less of a mental strain. On the other hand, wherever the body was left free to be governed by the reflex centers, it was found that the mind was rested and the person enabled to recuperate after a hard day's work. In a game, the movements of the person are dictated not by the will but by the eye or ear through some center which controls the muscles, and the movement and all connected with it is perfectly spontaneous.

About this time, in the training school at Springfield, the question was thoroughly discussed in a physical department meeting, and the conclusion reached was that recreation, as found in games, was the best means of giving physical exercise and brain rest. The senior secretarial class at this time included a large number of business men who had experience in the business side of life and looked at things from a practical standpoint. The faculty had decided that these should spend at least one hour per day in physical work, mainly for the sake of their health. This time was occupied with the ordinary routine of the gymnasium and it appeared to them like a task, except to the few who appreciated the benefit that it might be in future life to have a knowledge of this subject. At the faculty meeting in which the question of recreation was discussed, it was decided to try the effect of recreative work upon these men. Accordingly, at the close of the meeting the superintendent of the department assigned the writer to this part of the work saying, "See what you can do with them." Accordingly all the well known games were looked up and introduced into the gymnasium, some of them being modified slightly to suit the circumstances; each game was played for a short time with interest, but soon it seemed to lose its charm. Thus it seemed as if recreation was not the thing that was best adapted for this work. But, upon looking the games over it appeared that each one, while having many good qualities, still lacked some element which kept it from being a perfect game for these conditions. Accordingly the next attempt was to select and adapt some game for the gymnasium that would fill the required conditions. But none seemed to offer. Lacrosse was difficult to learn; football was rough, and could not be modified so as to suit the gymnasium. The only resource, then, was to make a new game that would fill the place. Certain conditions had to be met, and these were formulated and one after the other used as a standard to gauge the game as it grew. The conditions were as follows: First, it must be interesting in itself; second, it must be easy to learn; third, it must be such as could be played indoors and in any kind of a gymnasium; fourth, it should be as free from roughness as possible; fifth, it should accommodate a large or small number of men; sixth, it should give an all-round development; seventh, it should be scientific enough to be interesting to old players.

That there should be a ball of some kind was the first point settled upon, because by this means the game could be made scientific and interesting, bringing in the element of physical judgment, and yet be free from the personal contact which is so often the cause of roughness. A large ball was used in order that it might be handled with the hands and not be hidden and required no practicing with stick or bat. Thus any person would play the game without practicing, making it peculiarly suitable for men who did not care to spend time to acquire the game and yet wanted the recreation and exercise.

The next question was how to prevent roughness. The popular games were scrutinized to see wherein their roughness lay. The foundation of this in Rugby is the tackling, and this is necessary in order to get the ball from the opponent. In order, then, to eliminate this feature the person holding the ball was not allowed to hug it, or hold it with any part of himself except the hands. Furthermore, the person having the ball was not allowed to run with it, but had to throw it from the place in which he caught it; thus the necessity for tackling was done away with. In association football the roughness arises from the danger in kicking the ball, so that it was made contrary to the rules to kick it. All checking was also eliminated as being likely to lead to roughness. Again, as in many instances a person might be hitting at the ball and miss it, striking his opponent, and as this might be taken as an excuse to pay off an old score, the players were forbidden to use their fists in striking the ball. Furthermore, any personal attack was forbidden, holding, striking, tripping and such personal attacks on the opponent.

In all games where the opening of the goal is vertical, as it usually is in games, and the opponent stands to guard it, there is, of necessity, a great deal of swift passing and throwing, which, in a gymnasium, is likely to do damage to the apparatus and even to the players. To obviate this the goals were placed horizontally and at such a height that a player could not cover it and prevent the entrance of the ball. Then, in order to hold the ball that the referee might be able to assure the players that the ball had really entered the goal, a bottom of some kind was necessary to retain it inside. The first goals that were used were simply a couple of peach baskets hung one at each end of the gymnasium and from this the game takes its name.

Basketball was thus made in the office and was a direct adaptation of certain means to accomplish certain ends. The rules were formulated before it was ever played by anyone; they were typewritten and hung up in the gymnasium before the game was started that the players might know what to do.

One day, before the class hour, the baskets were hung up ready for use, and when the class came upon the floor there was quite a little wonder expressed as to what these were for. At last some one suggested that it was a new game, and the tone of voice was by no means prophetic of success. However, they consented to try one more game, and, as it afterwards proved, the forlorn hope was the one that brought success. After the rules had been read, the ball was put into play, and from the time that it was first thrown up, the interest never lagged, not because of the science of the players, but because of the amusing positions and unexpected circumstances attending the progress of the game. It was not long until the rest of the students were standing in the gallery, looking on and thoroughly enjoying the fun. Thus it will be easily seen that the main interest in the game is due to the unexpected conditions which one is constantly meeting rather than to the competition which it affords. While the game may be made scientific, yet the science is only for the purposes of giving interest to those who have played for some time and are willing to spend time in acquiring the skill necessary to become expert. But when we reach that point where we sacrifice the true sport that is in the game and the development that it brings for the sake of glory, and of winning a game from some other team, then will it fail of the object for which it was first started.

Nothing more was done for a short time, but the local interest was so great that the players, in writing to their friends, so described it that some of the associations put it into practice before it was ever in print. In the February number of the *Triangle* it was first given to the public, and it was not long before it was played in a great many associations. It has been modified somewhat for the ladies, and to-day the ladies almost claim it as their game, and indeed it affords for them a game which is full of development.

Letter to Thomas Browne

April 7, 1898

A letter written by James Naismith to Thomas Browne on April 7, 1898, in which Naismith discusses the origins of the game. Browne was the first person who attempted to chronicle the game's origins.

Dear Mr Browne

Your letter reached me just as my final exams were beginning so that I have delayed answering till now. We finished up yesterday and will not know the results until tonight.

I shall attempt to give you the facts as nearly as I can and you can work it up to suit yourself.

It was in the session of 91 & 92. We had a class in the Sec'y dept that was composed principally of men who had been in business and were accustomed to look on the practical side of everything. They had been trained in all sorts of athletics and gymnastics until they thought they had enough and they began to rebel on having to spend an hour every day in the gym jumping over the horse and straddling the bars. When they got restive the question then was, is our work of the right kind to interest men?

About this time there was a revolt against the introduction of swedish educational gymnastics to take the place of the children's recess in the public schools. This led to the question of games.

At a meeting of the phy's dept held in Dr. Gulick's house (I think it was before the Christmas holidays), the question was brought up as to what constituted a good game and it was agreed that so far as the development of the right type of manhood was concerned Lacrosse was the ideal game. Then we talked over the different games and their good points and defects, and a strong desire that there was a game that would fill the requirements.

I happened to remark that I did not see why there could not be a game gotten up that would be all right. So Dr. Gulick said go ahead and see what you can do, and immediately turned over this class to my charge. I felt then that I had a white elephant on my hands but started in to do the best I could.

I tried all the games that seemed to offer any hope and studied each one, but the idea of lacrosse always in my mind. Then it occurred to me that the only way was to get one that would fill the requirements as nearly as possible. A large ball was easily handled, and stopping running would stop tackling and checking so that was the original thought which was developed into Basket Ball.

I sat down and wrote out 13 rules and had these typewritten and hung up in the gymnasium where the boys could read them. Then I got a couple of baskets (peach) and with the aid of Mr. Stebbins hung them in position at the ends of the gym.

When the class came down it was with a flutter of the heart that I watched the way in which this venture was going to take.

The first words were not very encouraging when one of the class made the remark, "humph! a new game." I asked the boys to try it once as a favor to me to see if it would not work. They started and after the ball was first thrown up there was no need for further coaxing as my work was finished and the boys did the rest. It was carried by the boys to their homes and spread from that point. Ruggles can give you an account of the first games that were played both in the school and outside.

You will see that the aim of the game to develop the man and not to make money or even to draw a crowd & while the latter objects are good yet I feel that the other ought to be chief purpose for which the game should be played.

I shall probably write you again about the rules as I thought of several things that might be slightly changed, and would add to the clearness of the rules.

Do not print this as it is but work it up to suit yourself and any further questions that you may ask I shall be glad to answer you.

I remain yours
Sincerely
J. Naismith

Thomas Browne Letter

August 4, 1943

A letter written by Thomas Browne to Springfield College stating that he has found the 1898 letter Naismith wrote him about the game's origins.

Dear Sir:

In cleaning up my attic I have discovered a letter from James Naismith today about the invention of basket ball. He had written to me when I was a student at Springfield College writing a history of the game. This you have as a graduate thesis of mine.

This letter of Naismith's will be of value as an original source especially since the death of the writer (the red marks were made by me when I was quoting portions in an article I wrote about that time).

I think I shall be sending some old publications of about the same time.

Very truly yours,
T.J. Zender-Browne
'98

Basket Ball 1914

This was a speech James Naismith presented at the Eighth Annual Conference of the National Collegiate Athletic Association (NCAA). It was later published in the *American Physical Education Review*, May 1914. This was then reprinted as a YMCA pamphlet, *History and Development of Basketball.*

It appears to be generally conceded that no paper on physical education is quite orthodox unless it traces its descent from the period of Greek culture, but I assure you that I shall not follow that precedent, for basket ball, unlike the great majority of our games, is not the result of evolution but is a modern synthetic product of the office. The conditions were recognized, the requirements met, and the rules formulated and put in typewritten form before any attempt was made to test its value. These rules, as typewritten in the office, which are now in my possession, are identical with the rules as first published and remained unchanged for almost two years. Their first appearance, in print, was in the *Triangle*, the school paper of the Y. M. C. A. College at Springfield, Mass., in the issue of January, 1892, under the heading, "A New Game." In the twenty years of its existence the game has been carried to the ends of the earth, and it is to-day in all probability one of the most widely known and played of all games. Its popularity and extensive introduction are due primarily to three factors: first, there was an absolute need for such a contribution; second, it was founded on fundamental principles; third, it was produced in an international institution, which gave it a world interest.

Physical education, in the early nineties, was confined almost exclusively to gymnastics, derived from a twofold source, the apparatus work of the German, and the free work of the Swedish systems. Athletics as we know them to-day were little used in the work of a department of physical education, games hardly at all. About this time there was a growing interest in games because of their human interest and their adaptability to intercollegiate contest. There had been a steady growth in these since the seventies when intercollegiate sports really began, but they were largely outside the scope of physical education. Those individuals who in the fall season were interested in and took part in football, found that, in the winter, apparatus work was more or less tiresome and uninteresting, while the influence that it might have on the individual did not appeal to the youth who did not know that he had a stomach, save as a receptacle, nor a heart, save in a figurative sense. This left a period of physical inaction for a great many persons who enjoyed participation in a wholesome form of competition. Basket ball was introduced as a deliberate attempt to supply for the winter season a game that would have the same interest for the young man that football has in the fall and baseball in the spring. There was a place that ought to be filled and that apparently was filled by basket ball.

The first principle on which the game was based was that it should demand of, and develop in, the player the highest type of physical and athletic development. This type in the mind of the writer was the tall, agile, graceful, and expert athlete, rather than the massive muscular man on the one hand, or the cadaverous greyhound type on the other. This necessitated that every player should have approximately the same kind of work; that it should demand of him that he be able to reach, jump, and act quickly and easily. Lacrosse was the ideal game to develop this type, but it was impossible to use it or adapt it for an indoor game. But the sport that we sought should embody the same factors.

The second principle was that it should be so easily taken up that any individual could make a fair showing without a long period of practice. It was necessary, therefore, to have very little apparatus and that so easily handled that anyone might make a start. The conclusion was that it should be played with a large, light ball. The only ball that answered that description was the Association football, and the first rules said that the game should be played "with an ordinary Association football."

The third principle was that, on account of the size and varying conditions of the gymnasiums of that time, it should be possible to play the game on any ordinary gymnasium floor. It is interesting to note that it was first played by two teams of nine men each, on a floor 35 x 45, equipped with apparatus, and having a running track in the gallery.

The fourth principle was that it should be capable of being developed to such an extent as to hold the interest of the player when he had become expert in the fundamentals of the game. In other words, it must be capable of being played as a team game. It has been thought that this element is being overemphasized, but the game must have this quality in order to succeed. Indeed, it is the phase that is most interesting to this Association, as the scope of our work is intercollegiate athletics. That the game has the power to hold the interest of the expert makes its use as an intercollegiate sport possible.

With these principles in mind the several games were passed in review or tried out on the floor, but none of them seemed to meet the requirements. Football was too rough, so was Association football; baseball, lacrosse, and tennis were impossible at that time of year. Track athletics lacked the element of personal competition with a moving competitor, while the gymnastic games lacked the team element. It was plainly evident that there was a need for a new game.

The confident assertion that a game could be devised to meet these requirements was met with incredulity and a quiet assumption that the ideal could not be realized. At the same time ample opportunity was given to demonstrate the possibility of such an accomplishment, and the opportunity for testing it was supplied by a class of young men who were compelled to take gymnastic work one hour per day, and whose frame of mind was such that a strike was the only outlet for the natural feeling—and basket ball was the result.

A simple process of reasoning gave the clue that introduced a new element into the game and marks it from all others. This was so simple that the results are surprising. The roughness in football is due largely to tackling. This is necessitated because the opponent is permitted to run with the ball in his possession; therefore, if we eliminate the running, we eliminate the tackling and its consequent roughness. The first step was therefore to prohibit a player from running with the ball in his possession, but he was permitted to throw it in any direction, either to make a point or to pass it to a team mate. This at first sight seemed to take away the possibilities of the game, but when the individual was permitted to move about anywhere, so long as he did not have the ball, the game became spirited and kaleidoscopic.

Association football was rough because of the fact that the ball is kicked through a goal, and the more forceful the kick, the greater the probability of scoring. This would be equally true if the ball were thrown through a goal. To eliminate this form of roughness, it was necessary to so modify conditions that in order to make a goal the ball should be thrown with care rather than with force. A change in the position of the goal solved this problem, for if the opening of the goal were horizontal and above the head the ball would have to be thrown with a curve and this source of roughness would be disposed of.

On asking the janitor for a box of about eighteen inches in width, he informed me that he had a couple of large peach baskets. These were fastened to the gallery for goals and from these the name basket ball was derived.

Another difficulty remained unsolved, how to start the game without kicking or scrimmaging. A solution came from Rugby, where, when the ball goes out of bounds, it is returned by throwing it in between two lines of players. Then in order to avoid the scramble for the ball, which generally ensued, it was decided to throw it up between two men selected for this purpose. Kicking and hitting the ball with the fist were prohibited from the first. With the elimination of running with the ball, there was no excuse for any personal contact, so that all manner of holding or handling the person of an opponent was absolutely prohibited. This has been a point of conflict ever since, but, according to the fundamental idea, there should be no doubt as to the proper attitude toward this feature of basket ball.

In two weeks from the time that the task was undertaken, the game was ready for its trial, and it was with a good deal of anxiety that I anticipated the outcome. The first exclamation by a bystander upon seeing the baskets was far from encouraging—"Huh, a new game!"—and under this caption it appeared in the *Triangle*. It was not until some time later that, in a conference with this same man, it was decided to call the game basket ball, and in the first issue of the "Guide" it was so called.

ITS DEVELOPMENT

The development of basket ball has been along three main lines. First, the rules were adapted for amateur teams, in an attempt to make the game beneficial to the players, while encouraging legitimate competition for the interest of the men and the organization, rather than for the benefit of the spectators. For this class there have arisen two sets of rules, the A. A. U. and the Collegiate, differing only in one essential, namely, that in the latter the player may make a play after dribbling, while in the former he is retrained. There was need for a divergent set of rules so long as there was a difference in the size of the courts, but as soon as the fields are large enough to admit of the dribbles, there will be no reason why there should be two sets of rules covering the same field.

The second group is that of the purely professional, where the rules are made for the spectator rather than for the player. This has been developed in and around Philadelphia, which is the home of professional basket ball. The professional game was developed through the reluctance of the Y. M. C. A.'s to give time and space to the sport, in the regular work of their gymnasiums. The players who had become expert and were enthusiastic over the game organized teams outside of the Associations, and thus the professional teams began. The aim of their rules was to make the game as fast as possible, for the sake of the spectators; the players are enclosed in a cage so that the ball never goes out of bounds, at the same time giving more space for the spectators. However, this has had the effect of slowing the game, as there are so many occasions for a held ball.

A third line of development was the introduction of changes to adapt the game to the characteristics of girls. The game was played at first according to the rules used by boys; but a misinterpretation of the diagram, illustrating the floor, by some of the Western institutions, gave them the idea of dividing the court into three parts. This avoided the danger of overexertion and exhaustion, which would naturally result when running from end to end of the field was permitted.

A second change was one intended to prevent any opportunity for a struggle over the possession of the ball. Therefore, a rule was formulated that whoever first got possession of the ball with both hands was allowed three seconds in which to dispose of it.

Thus at the present we have these four sets of rules. It seems to me a good provision that the different classes of players should have a game adapted for their own needs; but where the condition of the players and the grounds is similar, there seems little use for more than one set.

ITS DISTRIBUTION

The distribution of basket ball has been along several lines. The first organization to take it up was the Y. M. C. A. This was natural since it originated in their Training College, and it was carried by the students to their home Associations, thus attaining an international scope. One of the players on the first team went to India, another to China, another to Japan, while others carried it over the United States and Canada. The first team was scattered over the world, carrying the game with them. The drawings for the first copy of the rules were made by a Japanese, who later went to his home country. Ever since, the Associations have been the great exponents of the game, and to-day it is played in most of the Associations of the world.

According to statistics supplied by Mr. Ball, one of the international secretaries, there are in the United States 1037 representative teams playing the game. There are a total of 5773 organized teams reported, which would make about 40,000 persons playing organized basket ball. And, if we include the Associations that use basket ball as an adjunct to the regular physical work, the estimate of Mr. Ball is 150,000 members who play the game.

In February, 1892, just one month after the first appearance of the game in the school paper, we find that it had been adopted as a part of the physical work in the Elmira Reformatory, and was used as a recreation and development for the inmates. It is, to-day, recognized as a useful adjunct to the physical and moral education of the youth in these institutions. Hon. H. W. Charles, of the Kansas Industrial School, writing of the game says: "Inasmuch as the inmates are usually lacking in physique and control, much stress is laid on those exercises which will correct these defects. I do not hesitate to commend basket ball as one of the most valuable factors in remedying these conditions."

The first educational institution to introduce basket ball was Carroll Institute, of Washington, D. C., as it was played there in February, 1892, or less than one month after it appeared in print. Cornell was the first college to use the game as a recreation, and there also it was first prohibited. So many men were playing on each side that, in their efforts to get the ball, fifty men would rush from end to end of the gymnasium, and the apprehension that it would do damage to the building led to its prohibition as a class recreation.

Yale was the first college to send out a representative team, as the Yale team played when they had to meet other institutions than colleges. In 1896, Pennsylvania, Wesleyan, and Trinity were playing the game and had representative teams. The University of Iowa was the first of the Western colleges to make it an intercollegiate sport. About the same date Nebraska University was playing the game. Kansas sent out its first representative team in 1898. Since then the spread in the colleges has been rapid, until to-day there are few colleges that do not have a representative team.

In the Army there are teams at the different forts, Leavenworth having twelve teams, Fortress Monroe nine, and others having representative teams. In the Navy, thirteen ships have teams which play whenever they have an opportunity, and this is encouraged by the Y. M. C. A.'s wherever possible. In the Canal Zone, there have been teams playing inter-city games, and last year there was a league of five teams playing the intercollegiate rules. In South America it is obtaining a foothold, and leagues are being formed in the different countries.

The spread among the high schools has been very great, especially in the West, where the state universities have encouraged it by holding an annual tournament. Nebraska University had a tournament in which there were fifty teams; Kansas held one in which there were thirty-three boys' teams and seventeen girls' teams; Washington, one with ten; Montana, one with twenty-nine; and Utah, one with thirty-three teams. These figures do not represent all the teams that played the game, but only those that felt that they had a chance of winning the tournament.

Basket ball is especially adapted for high schools, as it develops those traits which should be developed at that time of life. It is individualistic and at the same time it encourages coöperation; it develops the reflexes which must be developed at that time, if at all, in the ordinary individual. It can be played with few men and is inexpensive.

Another phase of the work is in the Sunday school leagues, chief among which is the league in Springfield, Mass., managed by the Training School. This phase is extending to other cities; Kansas City has a league of sixty-five teams.

In the playground, it has found one of its most fruitful spheres, as it interests more individuals, with less oversight, than any other game. In the New York Park Playground there are 300 teams organized. Foreign countries are organizing teams and playing the game either in connection with the Y. M. C. A.'s, schools, or colleges.

The game had hardly been well started before the girls saw its possibilities for their use. A company of school teachers in Springfield, Mass., organized two teams and played the game in Armory Hill Gymnasium. The game was illustrated at a convention in Providence, R. I., and it was carried to some towns of New England. Smith College early took it up and played it as an interclass game. The students going out from that institution spread it over the country, and in 1894 it was used in Wolfe Hall, a ladies' seminary in Denver. From this institution it spread to the high schools of that city, and soon there was a league organized. In 1896, the girls of Leland Stanford met a team from the University of California.

The schoolgirls of the Philippines are using it as a class game, and it is recognized by the authorities as one of the school interests.

In a recent work on the customs of Japan, basket ball is mentioned as one of the forms of recreation and development for the Japanese girls. The girls of China, even some of them with their crippled feet, play the game in that country. Australia has a league of girls' teams playing a series of contests. In England the girls of Oxford University play it as an outdoor sport.

In our own country the game is popular with the high school girls, and it forms one of the few games that they can use for recreation and competition. There is objection to the game when used as a spectacle for the girls' teams, but it is rapidly assuming its true place in the education of the girls. In one high school of Brooklyn there are thirty-two teams playing interclass games, and they are given a definite time on the day's schedule. Smith College has consistently used it as an intramural sport. The game as played by these institutions is the modified game for the girls, and this adds to its permanence and usefulness.

To see how basket ball appeals to and encourages the type of athlete set up as an ideal at the inception of the game, it is interesting to note the charts of the basket ball players. For this purpose I have introduced a chart showing the average measurements of the men who have earned their letter in basket ball at the University of Kansas. The player is about a 70 per cent man, symmetrical with the exception of the left arm, which is slightly smaller than the right. When compared with the ideal athlete of McKenzie, he is one-tenth of an inch taller and ten pounds lighter. The chest is not so muscular, but is flexible. This was to be expected as a development from a game that demanded so much from the lungs and heart. It is impossible to show the development in physical judgment, skill, and control, and those attributes which go to make up the ideal athlete.

	(A)	(B)	(C)
HEIGHT	69.1	72.9	72.4
WEIGHT	149.0	168.0	149.0
NECK	14.1	14.5	14.3
CHEST (CON.)	33.7	34.2	34.8
CHEST (EXP.)	36.8	38.8	38.7
WAIST	29.9	31.6	29.0
RIGHT ARM	10.5	10.9	10.2
RIGHT ARM UP	11.9	12.3	11.4
RIGHT FOREARM	10.5	11.3	10.5
LEFT ARM	10.2	11.0	10.1
LEFT ARM UP	11.4	12.4	11.2
LEFT FOREARM	10.2	11.1	10.0
RIGHT THIGH	21.2	21.8	21.0
RIGHT CALF	13.9	14.8	13.3
LEFT THIGH	21.0	21.9	21.0
LEFT CALF	13.9	14.9	13.3

Column A. The average of basket ball players of the University of Kansas.
Column B. The measurements of the captain of the University of Kansas basket ball team.
Column C. The measurements of the best all-round athlete of the University of Kansas
   (football, basket ball, track, baseball, and gymnasium).

BASKET BALL AS THE TYPE OF A COLLEGE GAME

It is intrinsically an open game, and exhibits skill rather than science. Audiences must expect to appreciate an exhibition of muscular activity, grace of movement, and immediate response to varying conditions rather than to see their team defeat the other. The game is enhanced by clean, rapid play, for it is then that skill can be shown, both in handling the ball and in intercepting passes by the opponent, so as to get the ball into the possession of the quicker team. It is not in a class with football, where the ball marks the progress of the game, and a partisan can become enthusiastic over a game, the science of which he knows nothing about. The main interest in basket ball lies in watching the activity of the players and the kaleidoscopic changes which take place. Every moment of a game is full of thrills, when expert players handle the ball. The instantaneous action of the reflexes, when a ball is caught, in deciding where it shall go, demands a great amount of coördination. There is not time to think out a play, but reflex judgment must control, and the action must be performed with lightning rapidity. No prettier sight can be found in athletic achievement than in a game where the ball, without any preconceived plan, passes from man to man in a series of brilliant movements and lands in the goal, or is cleverly intercepted when a goal seems inevitable. We watch such a game with an increasing admiration for the wonderful capacity of the human frame for accomplishing the seemingly impossible. No amount of rough work, even if it should result in a goal for our side, can compare with such a spectacle. It is indeed a narrow mind that puts goals before grace, scores before skill, or marks before manhood.

Institutions must sooner or later learn to judge the success or failure of a team as much, at least, by the manly attributes exhibited, as by the score. The problem of team games to-day is to discover some method of scoring that will include the attributes of skill and self-control.

One of the conditions that was thought necessary for the best kind of a game was that it should be capable of team work. This feature has been developed from the first, but there are two kinds of team work; *coöperative team work*, in which each player uses his team mates at the right time, and to the right extent, and has become so accustomed to doing this that he does not stop to think, but acts reflexly; *machine team work*, in which every man does that which he has been told to do and does it the same way every time.

Games differ in their capacity for one form or the other; e.g., Rugby is coöperative, American football, machine-like; lacrosse is coöperative, baseball, machine-like. Each of these has its own advantages. Coöperation develops the individual, machine play, the game; the former develops the general reflexes, the latter specializes; the former makes the player broad and independent, the latter makes him a cog; the former develops initiative, the latter, subordination; the former makes him depend on his own resources, the latter makes him dependent on the coach.

Basket ball has possibilities for both forms, but up to the present the former has been emphasized. There is a tendency to develop the machine type, but the effort of the Rules Committee has been to minimize this and to lay the main stress on the development of skill and initiative, the result of which will be the development of the spectacular rather than the partisan form of competition.

Games are instinctive, and intended to develop the individual for the business of life. The educational value of a game, therefore, should be judged by its effects on the powers of the participant. If it makes him better able to master the circumstances of life it is a benefit; if it hinders this, or if it is of negative value in this respect, then it cannot justify its place in a college program. The sports of early times developed brute strength and physical endurance, but neither of these is necessary for the college man after his graduation. But there are many factors that can be developed that would make him a better man and a better citizen. The attributes that are demanded in the life of the twentieth century are initiative, activity, quick judgment, adaptability to conditions, self-control, perseverance, and concentration. These are the attributes developed by basket ball. It is therefore a means of education.

Basket ball is one of the games that attract the player, apart entirely from the competitive element. It is one of the games in which a small group will work trying to make goals. There seems to be an attraction in endeavoring to put the ball in the basket, a desire to acquire the skill necessary to make goals, aside entirely from the feeling that you are doing better than someone else. Of course, the added interest that comes from a good contest makes it all the more attractive. It is this factor that makes it particularly adapted for interclass games and for the development of the individual. It is unnecessary to adapt the rules to suit the spectators, for it will be played wherever a goal and a basket are found. Even should it be put aside as an intercollegiate sport, it still has a part to play in the education of man. But the intercollegiate element is necessary to get the best out of the sport.

THE FUTURE OF THE GAME

The future of the game lies in the hands of the coaches and officials. The rules of the intercollegiate game are as nearly perfect as can be under the present conditions. Every safeguard against roughness has been introduced, in order to make the game as clean as possible. It is clearly within the power of the official to so enforce the rules as to make the game an ideal one, for the spectator as well as for the player. It is absolutely necessary that the game be kept free from objectionable features; first, because every play is right before the audience, and every act and even every word is within the range of every spectator. Any roughness therefore is immediately detected and becomes the subject of audible criticism. This is, in turn, heard by the players, and they feel that, if the official does not enforce the rules, they must themselves retaliate or be considered cowards, so that further roughness occurs and mars the game.

Second, the attitude of audiences towards the game is different to-day from what it was several years ago. Now everyone is looking for a square deal, and the official who does not give it is likely to hear from the audience. The official who does not rule as they think he should is condemned and brings the game into disrepute.

In a recent criticism of the rules there was a statement that it is impossible to play a defense, without playing the man rather than the ball. This is a shortsighted policy, as it is not necessary to keep the score small, for the scoring of goals is one of the interesting features to the spectators, and any score around thirty is not too large. In football there are from eight to twelve minutes of actual play, while in basket ball every minute, from the start to the pause for a goal or foul, is one of intense activity. Playing the ball does not mean that the opponent should be ignored, but that, instead of trying to keep him from scoring after he has obtained possession of the ball, a guard's object should be to prevent him from getting the ball at all. The latter calls for more skill than the former, for if the guard were allowed to hold the forward, it would be impossible to make points; but it would then be a tug-of-war, not basket ball.

Those who complain of the roughness of basket ball surely do not interpret the rules aright, for there is not a single provision that allows of any personal contact between players. How anyone can make a rough game of it and follow the rules is hard to understand. If any individual game is rough, the blame cannot be laid on the rule makers, for everywhere is emphasized the fact that the game should be kept free from personal contact in even the slightest degree. It is easy for an official to let fouls pass unnoticed for a time at the beginning of the game, and then endeavor to make the rulings strict after complaint has been lodged. It is infinitely better to be strict from the first, then the players will know what to expect, and will play accordingly. The officials should know the rules of the game and enforce them according to their letter and spirit, rather than according to the desire of any coach, manager, or audience.

In those sections of the country where the game has been kept clean, open, and free from roughness, it has grown in popularity and in esteem. But wherever the officials have been lax, or indifferent about the enforcement of the rules, the game has lost in popularity, and in some cases has been dropped because of its reputed roughness. In the Middle West, players and audiences have commended the work of the very strictest officials, while they have uniformly condemned the work of those who were lax, and allowed roughness to creep in.

The *responsibility* of the coaches is even greater than that of the officials, as many of the latter are influenced by the attitude of the coaches. When the coach lacks the knowledge or ability to perfect a team in individual skill, he is willing to permit holding, in order that his men may keep the score down. He may even request that fouls be overlooked; thus roughness is introduced, for which the rules frequently get the blame. Or the coach may refuse to accept an official who is known to rule strictly and in accord with the spirit of the game. Thus the official to retain his popularity frequently officiates as the coaches ask. I have been asked by members of this Association if there was not some way to change the rules so as to eliminate roughness. There is apparently only one way to meet this difficulty, namely, to have the officials responsible to a Central Board, to get the information from impartial sources rather than from coaches and managers. At the same time dissatisfaction on the part of the coaches could be weighed, and a just estimate of the work of an official could be obtained.

RESPONSIBILITY OF THIS ASSOCIATION TO BASKET BALL

While the Y. M. C. A.'s were the early pioneers who carried the game into many countries, this body is now largely responsible for its growth and development. Formerly, it was recognized as a factor in recreation and physical development, and later, as having a value as a means of inculcating ethical instruction. To-day, without losing any of its powers, it has become a part of our educational systems, and in many cases is being introduced into the school program. The teachers in the elementary and secondary schools are graduates of our normal schools and colleges, and the attitude towards the game which they have acquired from their *alma mater* is likely to be the one which they will bear to it when they are responsible for its conduct, whether professionally or incidentally. That college men have an important part in the development of basket ball is seen in such instances as that of Goodhue, who introduced it into Syria; Exner, who organized it in one of the districts of China; Alford and Overfield, who made it popular in Alaska; Gray, who gave it an added impetus in India; the engineers in the Canal Zone, and the multitude of college men who are controlling the game in our high schools and academies.

Therefore, while the immediate responsibility of this organization is primarily with intercollegiate contests, yet it should use every means to put basket ball, as well as every other sport, on such a basis that it will be a factor in the molding of character, as well as to encourage it as a recreative and competitive sport. This organization should take such measures as will result in a rigid enforcement of the rules as formulated, and encourage a manly respect for the rights of others. So much stress is laid to-day on the winning of games that practically all else is lost sight of, and the fine elements of manliness and true sportsmanship are accorded a secondary place. One great problem for this organization is the formulating of a system of scoring that will take cognizance of these traits of manhood or the development of traditions which will make it impossible for a college man to take advantage of an opponent, save in those qualities which the sport is supposed to require. The bane of basket ball to-day is the attempt to evade the laws of the game and even the rulings of the officials. There is no more reason why we should take an illegal advantage of an opponent in basket ball than that we should put our hand in his pocket and take his wealth. Few college men would take money or valuables from another, yet they are taught by the practices of our sports that it is not dishonorable to take an illegal advantage of another, if there is little prospect of being caught. To-day, a player hardly dares do the manly thing if it will mean a loss of points, lest he incur the ridicule of the bleachers and the sneers of his college mates. The man who does what he knows to be right, when he thereby fails to score points, too often incurs the wrath of the coach and the scorn of his team mates.

If athletics are to occupy the place that they might in the development of the college man of the future, they must take cognizance of the manly traits as well as of the development of physical skill and ability. This organization, composed mainly of faculty members whose interest is in the making of men rather than in the making of athletes, is the body to inaugurate such a movement. It should set the standard by which a sport is judged, and then, by education and, as far as possible, by legislation make the forward step in the development of intercollegiate contests.

As a member of the Basket Ball Rules Committee, I wish to say that that committee has done everything in its power to make the rules the very best possible. I believe that they are adequate to meet the situation, but their power is limited. While they may make rules of the very best, they have no power to enforce them, and each college is a power unto itself, and may make such provisions that the good of the rules is annulled. It is entirely within the province of this organization to take the next step in the development of an observance of the rules and the cultivation of true sportsmanship. If this body, composed of representatives of the great colleges of this country, and of representatives of the great athletic conferences of our colleges, should go on record as in favor of a rigid enforcement of the rules, clean sport, courteous treatment by players and spectators, and a fraternal spirit between college men, it would introduce a forward step in the intercollegiate contests. The field would be broadened, and a true conception of a college athlete would ensue when we would realize that a college contestant is primarily a gentleman, secondarily a college man, and incidentally a basket ball player.

Letter to Mr. Morgan

August 14, 1928

A letter written by James Naismith to Mr. Morgan on August 14, 1928, in which he provides information on his family's history and the game's origins. The letter was subsequently republished in *McGill News*, the quarterly newsletter of McGill University, in 1992.

OLD MCGILL

Before the Dream Team: *An Influence Other than Preaching*
The high-priced talent of the American Dream Team dazzled spectators at the Barcelona Olympics, but that was never the intention of the McGill seminarian who invented basketball. James Naismith wanted a good influence over the minds of the young. In this previously unpublished letter, Naismith tells of the rationale behind the sport. It was found in the archives of the Brockville *Recorder and Times* by managing editor Perry Beverley. We have reproduced the letter in its original form.[1]

Lawrence, Kansas
August 14, 1928

My dear Mr. Morgan:

It is rather interesting that the first request from Canada for information regarding basketball should come from Brockville, only a few miles from my Canadian home.

The games that contributed were English Rugby which I played at Almonte, and at the McGill University for six years. This game contributed the method of throwing the ball in from the side lines and up in the center. Lacrosse, that gave me the idea of placing the men in their positions on the field and in penalizing for a foul, as the first penalty was that the player was sent to the side lines until a goal was made.

Duck on the rock that I learned at Bennies Corners School gave me the idea of the horizontal goal. The three games that contributed most were games that I had played as a boy and were all Canadian games.

My home was in Almonte, Ont., and I attended the High School in that town, though I lived in the country about two miles from the town.

My father, John Naismith, came from Glasgow where he was a lad with his grandfather John Naismith. He lived with an uncle until he was apprenticed to a carpenter and later he became a builder.

My mother's name was Margaret Young, daughter of Robert Young of Ramsay. The family consisted of three children: Annie still living in Almonte, Robert died at 18 years of age, and self born in 1861 in Ramsay, Ont.

We move into Almonte and there my school life began. We moved to Havelock where Father was building a hotel. When that was completed he built a sawmill on the Ottawa River, and was planning to erect a furniture factory when he died of typhoid fever. Two weeks later our mother also died and the children returned to Ramsay to live with an Uncle, Peter J. Young, now living in Almonte. It was on his farm that I spent my summers while attending McGill.

When 14, I entered High School and spent one and a half years, when I took a notion to farm, and worked with my Uncle until 19 when I returned to take up my studies where I had dropped them. But the authorities thought best to put me back at the very beginning and this made me work so that I finished the school at the same time that I would have had I entered where I left off.

During school life Athletics of all kinds interested me and whenever there was an opportunity I took part in them. My progress was largely due to the work of the H.S. Prin. Peter

McGregor [who] spent recess and dinner hours preparing several students for matriculation exercises.

I entered McGill with the ministry in view, and took no part in athletics during my first year. Walking through the campus one day, in the early football season, where the team was practising, one of the boys was injured and there being no substitutes the call came for some one from the spectators to help out. I answered the call and on account of my strength acquired on the farm I was given the place and played on the team from that date, playing most of the time at center. Early in my course my attention was directed to the need for systematic exercise and I joined the classes in Barnjum Gymnasium where I later became instructor while making my way through Seminary.

My attention was directed to the fact that there were other ways of influencing young people than preaching, by several occurrences that took place in sports. In games it was easily seen that the man who took his part in the manly way and yet kept his thoughts and conduct clean had the respect and the confidence of the most careless. It was a short step to the conclusion that hard clean athletics could be used to set a high standard of living for the young. It was this that led me, on graduating from the seminary, to take a trip through the U.S. and Canada to find out the value of the many opportunities that were on hand. One of the places visited was school at Springfield, then holding its summer session. The enthusiasm of the men there showed that they felt the importance of their influence and the possibilities of making better men of their classes.

The next fall instead of accepting a position in the ministry I spent the year at the school with the intention of returning to Montreal to the Y there.

An offer coming from the School in Springfield to become an instructor in that institution, seemed to open up the larger field and I accepted the position. It was in this year that the task was assigned to me to [invent] a new game and the result was Basketball.

The enclosure gives a pretty good account of the steps as they took place.

1. I had decided that the new game must have a large ball like football.

2. Why not play football? Because it was too rough. Why was it rough? Because we tackle. Why do we tackle? Because we must stop the runner. Don't let him run with the ball and there is no need for tackling. This was the new principle that was needed and it was an innovation in ball games.

3. What kind of a goal will we use? A perpendicular goal magnifies the value of a ball thrown as hard as possible, again roughness. In Duck on the Rock we often threw the ball in a curve and it did its work. Make the goal horizontal and they will be compelled to throw it gently. Raise it above their heads and there will be no fighting around the goal.

4. Eliminate all contact between the players and it will make it a game of skill rather than of brute force, no pushing, striking and &C.

5. How to put the ball in play to start the game.[?][2] Lacrosse and hockey started between two players, but it was impossible to let them fight for the ball and avoid roughness. In English Rugby when the ball went out of bounds it was thrown in between the forwards and the thought came why not throw the ball up between two players so that they would have an equal chance to get it.

6. How [to] penalize foul play?[3] Give one warning and if again guilty send him to the side lines until another goal was scored.

These fundamental factors were incorporated into 13 rules and were posted on the bulletin board before the game was played at all.

Most of these principles are still the large factors in basketball.

1. No running with the ball.

2. The horizontal goal up in the air.

3. No rough personal contact.

4. The method of putting the ball in play.

The game started in 1891 and it is estimated that 15,000,000 persons are playing the game today. The rules are translated into Spanish, Portuguese, French, Chinese, Turkish, and probably other languages.

I have hastily written this out as data for you to work up as suits you, and hope that it will be what you want. I will be glad to elaborate in any way you suggest.

Two years ago I travelled overland with my wife and two children to my old home in Almonte. I was delighted with the way that Canada had recovered from the severe drain on her men and resources, occasioned by her splendid response to the war summons. Wishing you every success I gladly respond to a call from a McGill Man.

Most sincerely yours,
James Naismith, AB McGill 1887

How Basketball Started and Why It Grew So Fast

1931

> This lecture, "How Basketball Started and Why It Grew So Fast," was presented as one of the Wingate Memorial Lectures of the 1931–32 season. It later became a chapter in *Aims and Methods in School Athletics* edited by E. Dana Caulkins in 1932.
>
> Also in the Springfield College Library Collection is a letter from E. Dana Caulkins, chairman of the Wingate Lectures, inviting a local basketball coach to bring his players to the lecture to help Naismith demonstrate teachings and movements on the court that he outlined for his audience.

Wingate Memorial Foundation
Office of the President
57 East 56th Street
New York City

Directors
Gustavus T. Kirby, President
George Albert Wingate, Secretary
S. R. Guggenheim, Treasurer
William J. O'Shea
Arthur S. Somers

Telephone: Wickersham 2-4580

December 9, 1931

Mr. George Barclay
Basketball Coach

Newtown High School
Chicago Ave. and Gerry St.
Elmhurst, L. I. NY

Dear Mr. Barclay:

It is fine of you to arrange to have your team assist in our lecture-demonstration program on Saturday morning, December 19th. I have arranged so that we can have our program in the gymnasium at the New York University, School of Education Building, Washington Square S.E. At ten a.m. Dr. James E. Naismith, who invented the game of Basketball forty years ago, will speak. A little before eleven o'clock I will introduce you.

I suggest that you assume that you have before you a group of teachers all of whom have just been given the responsibility of organizing and coaching a high school basketball team and that this is a new experience for all of them. You can include a discussion of organization and management, beginning with a call for candidates and ending with the close of the season. Also, I suggest that you outline your program of training and coaching beginning with your instruction as to diet and preliminary conditioning and ending with the last practice session before the final game. I suggest that you plan to finish your remarks at about 11:25 and leave ten minutes for answering questions. At 11:35 o'clock I would like to have you take the floor with your team (the seating in the gymnasium will be so arranged that adequate playing space will be available at one end of the gymnasium). You might plan your demonstration to illustrate the various methods used by you in your coaching throughout the season. However, of course I want you to be free to handle this as well as your speaking program in whatever way you feel will be most effective.

Of course, I shall make arrangement with Mr. Nathan Tillam so that the boys will have an opportunity to change their clothes and to take a shower immediately following the demonstration. I suggest that they bring their own towels.

Thank you for your willingness to help and looking forward to meeting you at ten a.m. Saturday, December 19th.

Sincerely yours,
E. Dana Caulkins, Chairman
Wingate Memorial Athletic Lectures

"HOW BASKETBALL STARTED AND WHY IT GREW SO FAST"
Dr. James Naismith (Originator of the Game)
"BASKETBALL COACHING FOR HIGH SCHOOLS"
George Barclay

The seventh of a series of lectures under the auspices of the Public Schools Athletic League was held at a School of Education of New York University, in the Gymnasium, Saturday, December 19, 1931, at ten-ten o'clock, Mr. E. Dana Caulkins presiding.[1]

CHAIRMAN CAULKINS: I can well remember my own first contact with the game of basketball in a small community not very far from New York City. It was announced in the papers there would be a demonstration of the new game—basketball. I think this was about the year 1898. We went out. It was played outdoors in a field by a group of young women. I can see that picture of those young women playing just as clearly as though I had seen it yesterday, looping the ball high from side to side, running about ten steps and stopping. Then the girl on the other side looping it back, running ten steps and stopping.

I was thinking this morning, "What a marvelous development that game has had since those primitive days of its creation."

We are very fortunate, of course, to have with us today the man who was the inventor or the originator of basketball. I suppose he feels that it is one of his children, and it is natural for while it has grown far beyond his control, at the same time during all these years, I know that he has followed the development of the game and helped in the changes of the rules, studied it and thought about it probably more than anybody else. That is only natural. I know that if you or I had invented the game, we certainly should have done the same.

Following Dr. Naismith's address, we are going to bring the game of basketball down to close quarters as it is played in New York City. Of course, in the discussion of all these games and sports, before we get through we try to deal with the practical problems that we are facing here under the conditions in New York City. So Mr. George Barclay, coach of the Newtown High School, and the players of the Newtown High School team will assist in the latter part of the program.

There are many millions who are indebted to Mr. Naismith for the painstaking, laborious work which he undoubtedly did in bringing into existence this game of basketball. We are delighted to have him with us here today. Dr. Naismith! (Applause)

DR. JAMES NAISMITH: Mr. Caulkins, Fellow Directors—as I understand, most of you are physical directors: When I go out and make a very elegant speech to my way of thinking, no matter what I say, at the close of the meeting there are always two questions that are asked me. So, in order to clear the atmosphere, I will mention those two and speak on them for a few moments at first.

The first question that is always asked, I don't care whether it is a group or whether it is a single individual, is this: How do you come to think of it? It seems to be a question in the mind of the individual as to how a person could think of a game of this kind.

The second question is, "What changes have taken place since the game first started?"

Allow me to give you just an idea of the conditions and the circumstances under which the game came into existence. There were two statements that I made that I feel were responsible for a change in my life. One was at a seminar in psychology conducted by the late Dr. Luther Halsey Gulick, whom a great many of you knew and who was one of the leading pioneers of the physical work in New York City. After he left Springfield, he came here and developed a great deal of the work here. He was conducting the seminar; during that seminar he made this statement, "There is nothing new under the sun, but everything new is simply a recombination of the factors of the already existing things."

We had been discussing for some time the necessity for a game for the winter season and thinking the matter over, I said to him, "Well, Doctor, if that is true, if the statement that you have made is true, then we can invent a new game."

Nothing more was said of it for a while and we went away. By and by at a faculty meeting, Dr. Clark, who is now in Springfield, had a class of secretarial men, men who were mature, who were more or less well developed, but they had to take an hour's work every day in the gymnasium, and the work that we had was calisthenics and apparatus work and work of that kind. The man who had had the class at first failed to interest them. Dr. Clark also said at the meeting that he found it difficult to keep the class interested in the work.

I again made a statement that got me into trouble. I said, "The trouble is that you are giving these mature men work for development rather than for recreation. They don't want development. They are not training to put this into practice or anything of that kind; they want recreation. If you would give them some sort of recreative work, it would be all right."

Nothing more was said for a little while until by and by Dr. Gulick leaned over to me and said, "Naismith, I want you to take that class." If ever I tried to beg out of anything, I tried to beg out of that. I was teaching boxing and wrestling and swimming and several of the things I enjoyed. I said, "No, I don't want to do that. I would rather do the work I am at."

"Well," he said, "I want you to do it."

There wasn't anything else for me to do but to accept the situation. I didn't say anything. But as we were walking out along the hallway, Dr. Gulick who was about three or four inches taller than I am, stooped forward and said, "Naismith, now would be a good time for you to invent that new game you spoke of," referring back to the statement I had made.

Well, I felt sort of insulted and sort of mad because he had given me this class of irreconcilables and I was just on my toes and I felt my fist closing and I looked up. I was looking for a good place to land that fist because when he gave me the one, he insulted me, and when he gave me the second, he added insult to injury. That is the way I felt at the time. But I saw a peculiar little glint in his eye as much as to say, "Put up or shut up," and I accepted the challenge. I had to do it, there wasn't anything else for me to do. I didn't want to do it. I fought that thing just as hard as anybody could fight it.

I went to work with this class. I tried the game of soccer and we smashed all the windows. I tried the game of lacrosse, trying to modify some of these games so they could be used—I smashed most of the fellows' arms. We tried rugby football and we finished the students up, until they were ready to quit on recreative games.

It was coming about the time when I had to report back to the faculty that I also had failed, and that is not a pleasant thing for any man to do, and I thought very seriously about it. Sitting at my desk and running my fingers through my hair, I began to question like this: "Why is it they all like football but why is it that we can't adapt it? We can't adapt it; it is too rough. It is too rough because we tackle. We tackle because the fellow runs with the ball. If he didn't run with the ball, there would be no necessity for tackling."

I snapped my fingers and said, "I have it."

That was the first new principle that we got in the game, that when a man received the ball in his hands, he had to stand still and dispose of it in some other way. Then the next question was, "What is he going to do with it?"

This was all done while I was sitting at my desk with a piece of paper in front of me, just asking myself these questions.

What are you going to do with it now? If you don't let them run with it, they have to do something with it. A man can't stand there and hold it and he can't just simply throw it haphazardly; you have to have some sort of a goal.

Then I thought of lacrosse. That was the game I had played as a boy. Unlike a good many of you who have the national game of baseball, the national game in the country I came from, Canada, was lacrosse. Thinking of lacrosse with its goals, I thought of the goal keeper and I knew that whenever we wanted to make a goal, the harder we could throw the ball, the more power we could put into it, the more chance there was for making a goal. Then I thought, "That won't do, because when I get that ball, I will smash it and that will make for roughness."

I had played a game way back in the country school called duck-on-the-rock, I don't know whether any of you ever saw it or not. It is a mighty fine game for recess in the country. There is a big rock out here—there was one about four feet high, and each fellow had a stone about the size of your fist. One fellow put his duck on the rock and we tried to knock it off and when we went to get our duck, then he could catch us as long as his duck was on the rock. I can remember throwing that rock as hard as I could, thinking if I struck his rock, it would go way down here and I would have a chance to come back. We weren't very old, but we were thinking of the inertia of matter at the time.

On the other hand, sometimes we would throw just a little bit of [a lob] and if it struck his rock, it put his over [there and] brought mine out here, and I came out and picked it up and [put it] back. I said, "What is the objection now to making the goal horizontal instead of vertical? Then they must necessarily lob the ball every time, instead of throwing it, as fast as possible for them to do."

That is the origin of the horizontal goal. I have been asked a great many times why we didn't make the goal vertical as the other goals are. But that is the reason for it, in order that when an individual is trying to make a goal, he will throw the ball in the arc of a circle. Consequently, speed doesn't count.

Then I thought of having this on the floor, having a mark on the floor as we had in other games, and I thought, "Well, that won't do, because he could stand in the goal and we couldn't make a goal." Then I thought if we would put it up over his head, there would be no chance for him to interfere with the goal being made, once it has left the hands of the individual. That is why the goal is horizontal and why it is up in the air. Why it is ten feet high, I will tell you just a little bit later.

The next factor that came into existence was this: how am I going to start this game? Well, I thought of putting the ball in the center. I thought of polo. We put the ball in the center and let them rush from each end. I thought, "No, that won't do. That is more roughness." Then it occurred to me how I had played English rugby and whenever the ball goes out of bounds in English rugby, the two forward lines line up just opposite each other like this and the umpire stands with his back turned and he throws the ball over his head into the line somewhere; nobody knows where it is going to land. Then I thought, "Well, that might be a good scheme," and just at the thought of that I sort of winced with the old idea of what the fellow used to do, how he used to take his arm like this when I was coming down with the ball in my hand and caught me in the [pit of] the stomach. I thought that is more roughness.

Then I thought, "If I take two individuals and two only and throw it up between them, then I shall have done away with roughness." I didn't calculate on the ingenuity of the American young [men] because I have seen some roughness done even when there were only two at that point.

You will notice, some of the old guide books say [that the ball] must be thrown in such a way that it lands between [the two centers]. That seems superfluous under the present conditions, but at that time the referee didn't go on the floor at all, he stood out here on the side lines and tossed the ball so it came down between the two center men. The first that I remember seeing the ball thrown up in the center was in 1908 when the official stepped out on the floor and threw the ball up in the center. That probably was one of the first occasions, at least it was the first one where I had seen this.

The next thing was to put it into practice. We wrote out these thirteen rules. There were thirteen rules specifying what could be done and what could not be done. I have the copy of the rules, which is rather interesting.

About two weeks later, a young man came to me, a member of the class. He said, "You remember the rules you pasted on the bulletin board?" (because I had them typewritten and placed on the bulletin board.)

I said, "Yes."

He said, "They disappeared."

I said, "Yes."

He said, "I took them. I knew that this game was going to go and thought that would be a good souvenir, but I think you ought to have them."

He pulled them out and handed them to me and they are in my possession to this day, the original sheet of paper that was posted on the bulletin board with the thumb tack marks in the corners. I have always felt that that was as fine a piece of sportsmanship as I have seen for a while.

This same man came to me shortly after that and asked me, "What are you going to call this game?"

The first time it had been put in print, it was just simply labeled "a new game."

I said, "I don't know what we will call it."

"Well," he said, "how would it do to call it Naismith ball?"

I said, "No, that won't do; that is enough to kill any game."

Then he thought for a minute and said, "How would it do to call it basketball?"

I said, "That sounds good. We have a basket and we have a ball. We'll call it basketball."

That is how it got its name from this man, Frank Mahan, the leader of the incorrigibles.

After the rules had been written out and put on the bulletin board, I started down with a soccer football in my hand to start the game, to try it out. As I was going down, I asked the janitor of the building, "Have you a couple of boxes about eighteen inches square?"

He thought for a minute and said, "No, I haven't; but I will tell you what I have. I have a couple of old peach baskets down there about that size, if that will do you."

I said, "Bring them up."

So he brought them up and I took them and nailed one on each side of the gallery, one at this end and one at the other end. You know a peach basket is smaller at the bottom than it is at the top, consequently when we nailed it up, it sloped forward and in that case we had to shoot most of our goals from directly in front. A little later I will speak of the change that has taken place in the goal.

When the class began to assemble, as you can imagine, I was in a pretty nervous condition. I didn't know whether this was going to be a successor not. I hadn't any idea. Mahan came down. He had played tackle on the football team, a big burly fellow, and he happened to look up and saw a basket at one end of the gallery. Then he followed around, I kept my eye on him, until he came to the other end where there was another basket. He said, "Huh, another new game."

That just about sunk my heart, because I felt, "This is the attitude of the group, they are going to fight everything that is brought before them."

However, I threw the ball up between Mahan and Duncan Patton, another big, burly fellow, who played guard on the football team. I selected those two as captains because I thought I would get them to manage the team. I threw the ball up between them and I never had any more trouble with the class and I never had more trouble with the game. From the first time that that ball was thrown up, the class took to it. It wasn't two weeks until we had an audience of 200 people in the gallery watching the game every noon hour, because this class came from eleven to twelve-fifteen, and the people would come in to watch this new game.

From that time it has gone on of its own momentum, carried into all the different parts of the world, for two or three reasons. First, because it was gotten up in an international institution. We had men at the Y. M. C. A. training school from China, from Japan; one from France, Emil Theis; we had them from Nova Scotia, from all over the different parts of the world.

By the way, it is just forty years this month, just about this time, I think, when the first game was played. These boys took it back to their home towns and it began to go all over the country. So that we didn't have any more trouble with the class nor with the game.

There are a few things I wish to bring up. There are several fundamental principles in basketball and so long as those principles remain, it will be basketball. When we change those we had better change the name.

The first is that it requires a large, light ball as a soccer ball or as we have now, a basketball. It is a little bit larger.

Second, there is no running with the ball.

Third, the horizontal goal; and, fourth, no personal contact.

With those four fundamental principles, the game is basketball. They were all there when the game started and there are very few fundamental principles that have been added to the game since that time.

In football, we have changed a great many, added new principles from time to time, but in basketball I don't know of any real fundamental principle that has been added to it. The method of scoring goals and a few things of that kind have been modified and changed.

In sending to Mr. Caulkins some of the ideas that I had, he chose several of them and one of them was the place of this game in physical education. Has basketball a place in physical education? The superintendent of physical education in Missouri asked me one day, "I wish that you would come out in the papers with a statement that basketball is not adapted to children of the rural schools."

I said, "I can't do anything of that kind, because I don't believe it for a minute."

I believe it is as well adapted for the rural schools as it is for any place else and if you travel through the country, you will see a basketball goal up in almost every country schoolyard. I know you will in Indiana and Kansas. Coming along on the train, I looked into a back yard and there was a goal, made out of a few old pieces of lumber, a basketball goal in a back yard right down in the bottoms of, I think it was Syracuse, or some town like that. So that it has become a part of physical education.

The difficulty is that some people have made it all. I find that some physical educators, and I have seen them when I went to visit them, will say, "Yes, I have a class at so-and-so," and they may call the roll and they may not. Then they will say, "Where is that basketball," and throw out the basketball on the floor with forty boys and tell them to go to it. That is not the intention of basketball at all. Basketball is not a whole system of physical education. In the first place, basketball does not develop physique. That is one thing that we are neglecting.

It is rather interesting that a few years ago I was fighting for recreation; today I am fighting for the reverse of recreation. We have gone, in the United States of America, recreation mad. I don't mind in institutions outside of high schools or the school system where recreation is the thing, but inside of the school system we must build up a good physique in the individual or he won't be at his best.

I can remember very distinctly when my boy was growing up. I had been brought up on a farm, hard work. My father and mother died when I was nine years of age. I was brought up on the hard work of the farm. When I went to the college, I was stooped forward like this and my hands had the same position they have at the present time from handling the fork and the axe and the reins and so on, year after year.

I said, "My boy will never do that. I want him to be straight and agile and smooth."

Then I began to think, I was about fifty years of age at the time, I had never been sick, hardly knew what sickness was, and I said, "Why?"

"Well, you can blame it on heredity, you can blame it on a good many things, but I blame it or rather credit it to the hard work that I had to do as a boy." I wouldn't take a back seat for anybody when it came to forking hay or anything of that kind, until I had built up a physique, the strength of which I didn't know; I didn't know the limit of it.

Then I thought, "I can't afford to let my boy miss that thing."

I put him into tumbling, one of the exercises which I think is the very finest. The other day he won four chocolate sundaes or something of that kind of lifting one side of the front end of a Cadillac car. He is not a big man at all. He is not as big as I am. But we gave him that constitution and that power. I can't tackle him myself today, I have to cry, "Uncle," when he tackles me. But I feel I did a fine thing for that boy by giving him that kind of work while he was young and while he was growing.

The point is this: Up to a certain point in our school system we must look out for the development of the physique of the individual. We have gone to the other extreme of developing the skill. You know, Stanley Hall years ago said that if we build the superstructure without building the foundation, the individual won't be as valuable. In our school system we want to build the foundation, and after that add on this the superstructure of the skill and all these finer things that come to pass.

I wonder how many of you could go back, put yourselves back in 1890 where we didn't have any sort of competition at all during the winter season. We have grown up, you folks have grown up accustomed to basketball and accustomed to volley ball and accustomed to a number of these games. There are thirty of them that have been brought out since basketball came. We didn't have one of these then. The only thing we had was three deep and a few of those things, all group games; we didn't have a single team game with competition. That is the condition that we were in at that time.

As a result of that, we built up pretty fine individuals, put them into apparatus work and everything of that kind, but we didn't give them the very thing that is necessary—team competition.

I divide athletics or physical education into three classes: Gymnastics where we are dealing with the individual on a piece of apparatus or handling the piece of apparatus, athletic events where I am competing against an inanimate object. I take a shot and I see how far I can put it. I have a track and I see how fast I can run. I have a pole vault and I see how high I can go. I am competing against an inanimate object.

In a relay meet not long ago a young man came to me and said, "That hurdle isn't quite right."

I looked at it. I said, "I think it is." We got a tape line and we measured it and checked it for height and for distance, and it was exactly correct. When the boy ran the hurdle, he knocked it over. Why, I don't know. But he just had an idea in his mind that that hurdle should be a certain thing, and you know they will skin those hurdles two or three inches.

When you go out to play a game like basketball, you can't predict that man is going to be over there or this man is going to be over here. You have a human being with the same powers you have at these different points, and you have got to meet that. This is the thing that we didn't have in 1890, in the winter season. That is the place for basketball to come in, to give us that contact mind against mind, to give us that contest of individual against individual, and yet without personal contact.

You know volley ball is a business man's game. Why? Because here is a group, one team is on one side of the partition and another team is on the other, and they can't bat each other in the [way]. You see a group of business men playing baseball or basketball, [and they] want to get at each other, but they can't in volley ball.

What we wanted to [do was challenge them in] this contest, occupying the same territory and yet not making personal contact. That is where I feel basketball has a tremendous place in physical education, just in that field where we develop these different factors of the individual.

There is another thing that basketball does. At that time, where we had heavy apparatus work, that didn't develop the heart and lungs. Some of you older men may remember Dowd when he came out with his great muscular arm, and you will see it outlined on Blankey's "How to Get Strong," great muscular development, if you look in the magazines today, you will find Lindberg and Swaboda and a whole lot of these men have great, powerful muscular development. That is one phase of it, but that is not everything. We want to develop the heart and lungs. This man Dowd died of tuberculosis before he was through with his physical education.

Basketball gives us a chance to do that, not quite so seriously as a great many people seem to think, that you are moving from start to finish. It is not true. About 37 per cent of the time you are active, according to the stop watch. I have been watching this thing both in basketball and football for several years.

Another thing that basketball has done for athletics and physical education, it has changed the attitude of a great many people, especially church people. I can remember that when I played football on the university team (this was in Canada; I don't know whether it was the same thing here or not, it probably was) there was a little group of my chums that got together and prayed for me because I was playing on the football team. Can you imagine such a thing? Well, you know one of those same boys wrote me the other day and he made this statement, I consider it one of the finest things I know of, "Of all the boys in that class, I don't think anyone has made a bigger contribution to character building than the one who got up basketball."

The same fellow forty years ago prayed for me because I was playing on the football team and now he makes a statement of that kind. It just shows how things have changed.

Another factor that I think is a magnificent thing is the leisure, the use of leisure time. In Kansas City, for instance, we have 300 teams organized and playing regular games, Sunday School teams and institutional teams and things of that kind; 700 teams in the school system and a number of college teams outside of that. These are all organized. The majority of these 300 teams are spending their leisure time, and to me it is infinitely better for a group of young men or young women to be playing basketball or [even] watching activities like basketball than it is to be attending a theater or attending a moving picture show or even playing billiards or in any other resort that an individual can go to to occupy [his free time].

Another factor in physical education that I think basketball has brought, is this: Previous to that time we didn't have any games, but when they got the idea of how to make a game, then the physical directors of the country began one after the other to make new games, until we have today thirty-six games in which they are using a basketball, other games in which they are not using a basketball, but have gotten out to meet these particular conditions.

I suppose that one of the best illustrations is Dr. Clara Baer of Newcomb College, who got out a game there she calls Newcomb, just a modification of basketball. Captain ball and center ball and a lot of these are just simply modifications. To me that is one of the big things, bigger than having the game, the idea of putting into the minds of individuals the method by which they can meet these conditions.

Then as for some of the changes that have taken place, I mentioned a little while ago that the rules were written out and put on the bulletin board. I have here a copy of those rules and this is the first guide book that was brought out—not this book I have in my hand, but this little one inside. This booklet contains a copy of the first four guides, '92, '93, '94 and '95. That is the size of the four guides. This is the '31 guide. You can see the difference between the two.

There are only thirty-one rules in this little book here. In the first, there were thirteen rules. In the last book, there are 187 rules, footnotes, and so on.

One of the big things in the changes that have taken place is the change in the court. I don't suppose you folks realize where basketball was played. I never played it myself, naturally, except as a member of the faculty team. I have had my team play in all sorts of conditions, in a hall with a row of posts running down the center, the whole hall was only thirty feet wide with a row of posts running down the center, and the ceiling was eleven feet high. I have played in the loft of a livery stable. In 1901 we played in the loft of a livery stable while I was in the University of Kansas.

Today they are building tremendous great field houses and one of the factors in that field house is the accommodation not only of the players, the height of the ceiling and the things of that kind, but the accommodation of the spectators. I attended a final in the Indianapolis interscholastic at which there were 15,000 spectators. I came a little bit late to the game. I thought there wasn't any hurry. I had a seat ticket in my pocket and I had an official's badge on. When I came to the door, the doorkeeper said, "You can't get in."

I said, "I would like to go in, I have got to make a talk here in a few minutes."

He said, "It doesn't matter, you can't get in," and they wouldn't let me in until I called for the chief, and he let me in. There were 15,000 people in that hall and that was eight or ten years ago.

Now they are building field houses that will accommodate 20,000 and 30,000 to see a game. The floor is very different. We don't pick up slivers anymore under our finger nails.

The change in the goal. At first the goal was a peach basket. You can see this goal here is almost the shape of the peach basket, but it hangs out. The first change was made during the first year. It was made by Lew Allen of Hartford. He couldn't supply peach baskets enough because as the ball bounded against it, it wasn't long until the basket was broken up. He took a piece of woven wire about two feet in length and he wound that into a cylinder eighteen inches across and ran a few cords across the bottom of it and nailed it against the gallery. That added a new factor.

When the game became horizontal, when the top of it became horizontal, we could shoot from the side as well as from the front and it widened the scope of the game.

The Narragansett Machine people got out a goal something like this and there have been a great many different goals gotten out since. I like the goal personally that has a little bit of a stop, according to the rules, but we do find a great many like this and we find disputes coming out as to whether it goes through or not. As I look around, I see three or four different types of them here. You have one over there with the old leather bands on it, the type of goal that has been in use for a great many years.

The next change took place in the back stop. At first the goal was fastened against the gallery and the gallery didn't always have the ribs close enough so the persons couldn't get through and the spectators would lean over and as the ball was coming pretty close, they would help it in or if they were on the opposing side, they would give it a little touch and keep it out. These are actual facts. I have seen them performed. It is not myth or theory or anything of that kind. I have seen them reach out their hand and assist their team.

Well the next proposition was how are we going to keep them away? So we just stretched a piece of chicken wire across in front, and if you look back in some of the old guidebooks you will find it says there must be a wire screen behind the goal, but the goal was still fastened to it. As a result, the home team found how it worked. As a result, some of them went up and actually made a little groove running from this point down. So when the ball struck this screen, it would roll into the goal. (Laughter) This, of course, gave the home team quite an advantage. The rule at present is that the back stop must be of a flat surface. We got glass backstops for a [time] because in a gallery we had some of the spectators up behind and they couldn't see the most important part. When we put the glass back stops in, they could see just as well from behind as they could from in front, an excellent thing except the rules committee made the ruling that the back stop must be painted white. When you paint a glass back stop white, there is not much good in having the glass. So that we had the back stop as you have it here. At first it was six feet by six. Later it became six feet by four.

At first there were two officials, a referee and an umpire, and the referee's job was to watch the ball. He didn't have anything to do with fouls whatsoever. His job was simply to watch the ball and the umpire watched the men for fouls. But they found the umpire couldn't watch all the game, he was very liable to be right up where the ball was. So we added another umpire to it. We put two umpires in to cover that.

The next step was to give the referee the power of calling some fouls and there were some fouls, the fouls on the ball he could call, and the umpire called those on the back field. Later on we gave the referee the full power of calling any foul any place that he saw to and did away with the second umpire.

Another step that has been made within the last year (I don't know how much you follow it here, but we do in Kansas), we have an umpire on this corner and an umpire on that corner. He is responsible for anything that occurs on this end of the field and own about two-thirds of the way on this side. That field is his. The other umpire has the other part of the field and it works very nicely indeed, if you get two men of about equal status. The only objection we have is this: we have a man by the name of Quigley who is a baseball umpire during the summer and he is good and the other fellow simply lets him do all the work. But it works very nicely. As a matter of economy, however, this year we have eliminated the second official and simply make one man do all the work. It is simply a matter of economy. I don't know how it will work out; I don't think it will work out. The only thing that we can depend upon is that the fellows will play the game pretty square.

The penalties are another thing that has changed very materially. The first penalty was that three consecutive fouls count a goal. That was the first penalty. If you made a foul, your side made another and made another without the opposing team making one, that counted you one goal, the same as if you had made a goal. However, on personal fouls, we didn't use the word "personal," but the differentiation was there. In the case of striking, hacking, tripping or anything of that kind, the first infringement was a foul; the second disqualified the player, and he was put out of the game until the next goal was made. Then he could come back into the game. If, however, that was intentional, he was put out for the whole time of the game. We now have this thing all worked out, systematically arranged so we have the personal and the technical fouls and the violations and so on.

It was found that two points for the opponent was too much for three fouls because sometimes the game could be won by that, so that they made the goal from the field count two points and the penalty for three fouls count one point. It was found that that again was too severe on the individual and then was introduced the idea of giving him a free throw and the free throw line was put at twenty feet. From twenty feet they threw for the free throw. That again was found to work to a disadvantage to the team that was fouled. It wasn't penalty enough. They couldn't hit the goal often enough, so it was moved up to fifteen feet and it now remains at that point.

The number of players. In this class that I spoke of, there were eighteen players, eighteen in the class. We divided them into two. That left three forwards, three centers and three guards, a nice team. We used that for the first year, nine men on a side. In fact, one of the thoughts that we had in mind was that this game should be able to take care of a great number of people and we thought of filling the floor and putting the basketball in. They tried that at Cornell University, in one class there with 100. They started a basketball game after the class was over, but the trouble was the whole 100 men would run down to this goal, and when the ball went down there, the whole 100 men were down there. They got up so much momentum they threatened to drive the end out of the gymnasium and they called the game off.

The wonderful thing to me is this, that when we first played there were only a few gymnasiums in the city, I don't know how many you had in New York. I know in Kansas City we had only about three. Instead of getting a few teams with a large number, we have gotten to a large number of teams with a small number of players on each team. Instead of having 300 players, which we would have thought was tremendous, they now have 3000 playing in place of the 300. Evolution has brought that about that we meet the condition, but we meet it in very different manner from what we anticipated.

The advance in skill. There isn't very much use in my telling you anything about that. You know as much about the skill as I do. There is this, however: You can imagine, when that ball was first thrown up, who knew what to do with the ball. Well, I didn't, neither did any of the men. It was simply, "There is a goal and there is the ball; get it in it." That is all the coaching there was. We read the rules, threw the ball up and said, "Get the ball in through that goal," and, "You fellows get it in through there."

From that time there has been a tremendous development of skill and there isn't anything that thrills me quite as much as to see a fellow jump from the center, just tip that ball with the tips of his fingers, it goes to the other man, he touches it over to a third man and he puts it in the goal. I can't keep my seat when I see a thing like that. I always think, "Why on earth didn't we have a game like that when I was a boy so I could have become as expert in the same way."

There are one or two rather interesting things. The men were lined up with opponents, man to man, all over the floor. There were nine men. They played that way for a little while, until down here in 23rd Street, New York, there was a team that couldn't get together except twice a week, but those two fellows spent every evening from six to seven-thirty when the floor was vacant, the two of them, or the three of them, just practicing shooting goals, nothing else, no team work or anything of that kind, until they could make goals from any angle. As a result, when that team went out, they played twenty-nine games and won every one of them.

[A coach] out here in Passaic, not very far away from here, says that he works on the offense. He pays very little attention to the defense and he won 159 games straight. I am not quite sure of the number, but I think it is 159.

We in the West, however, have paid a little more attention to the defense.

When these men became so expert, man to man, there was a boy named Archiquette, of Carlisle, who came out to Haskell and played against our man we had coached to make goals, Fred Owens; and he could make them as fast as he could throw them. He couldn't make a single goal with Archiquette there, he could guard him so closely. The next game I put Owens in as a guard and Chet Smith up forward, who couldn't make a goal if he was lifted up on a ladder, and Archiquette followed that fellow all around the floor and Owens made goal after goal and we won hands down. Archiquette came to me and said, "That was a dirty trick you played on me."

I said, "Archiquette you are a guard, aren't you? Find a way to meet that proposition." And there is where your zone defense comes in. He would take the first man that came down, it didn't matter whether it was the forward, he was told to meet, or anybody else, and there we had the zone defense.

A little later, Cook of Minnesota (he is yet with Minnesota) away back about 1896 got the idea when the opposing team got the ball down there, he would send all his men down to that field to get the ball away, and whenever you get five men against four, you are going to get the ball. Then he would come up the field, passing the ball from one to the other, and they left one man there. It was five against four here and they won their games for a number of years in that way, until the other side got the idea as soon as their man got the ball, as soon as the opposing team got the ball, the whole five came down this way. It is very interesting to me to see a fellow run from that end of the field clear down under his own goal and maybe make a swipe at the ball as he goes by. Here is a man who has the ball in his hands and he makes a swipe, but keeps on running down, the five-man defense. I haven't very much use for the five-man defense. I think it is against the fundamental principles of basketball. Basketball is not a game where one individual has any right to the ball, and I have heard crowds yell at the man because he stood back there with the ball when these five men were crowded down here. If I had been playing the game, I would have sat down on the ball and said, "Come and get it."

They have the obligation to come out and get that ball; they are the ones that are delaying the game, not the man with the ball.

However, the five-man defense has its place and is being used to-day—but only at times. In the game I witnessed just the other night between the Kansas Aggies and Kansas University, about half of the game was played man to man and the other half was the five-man defense.

I don't know why Mr. Caulkins should be interested in the girls; I am, I have got three of my own. But he wants to know about the girls. Way back, just very shortly after the game started, there was a group of school teachers that came along past the door and they would come in and stand in the gallery and watch the game. They asked me, "Well, why can't we play that game?"

I said, "I don't see any reason you can't. I believe it would be a good thing."

They said, "Will you give us time?"

I said, "You can have the gymnasium at a certain time."

They came in dressed in their high-heeled shoes, bustles and their constricted waists and all the paraphernalia that went with the [female] sex at that time. They started to play the game. It wasn't very much of a game, as you can imagine, but they enjoyed it. They asked me one day, "We are going to have a game, will you referee?"

I said, "Yes."

I didn't know what I was undertaking. (Laughter) I started in. By and by I called a foul on one of the teachers. She came over to me and said, "Did you call a foul on me?"

I said, "Yes."

She told me all my history of the past and where I was going in the future. (Laughter) Do you know, I couldn't get rid of that girl? (Laughter) She was so interested in telling me about myself that I couldn't get away. I walked out to the middle of the floor and threw the ball up and she had to go back to her place. Why? Girls never had a chance to be sportsmen. They hadn't played any sort of a game. They were like the ministers. I refereed a baseball game between ministers and lawyers. (Laughter) During the game there wasn't anything under the sun those lawyers didn't call me, but the ministers never said a word. After the game was over, the lawyers would come up and pat me on the back and say, "You are awfully blind, but you did make a fairly good job of it."

The ministers all went away with a grouch. (Laughter)

Why? Because they hadn't had a chance at that time to practice sportsmanship.

But I will tell you, I have seen some of the finest sportsmanship among girls' teams. I saw the Commercial Grads, the team that toured Europe, made $11,000 and toured Europe and played every game they had out there, and finer sportsmanship I never saw in my life. The girls have become sportsmen. For that reason I think we ought to begin to modify the rules.

You know the old rule in the girls' game. She has three seconds in which to throw that ball. Why? Because if anybody took it away from her, she was going to tear their hair (laughter). That was the feeling she had.

I can remember refereeing one girls' game between Haskell, the Indians, and the University of Kansas. The Indian girls stood over like this, or rather they stood right over, overguarding. One of them came right up with her head and struck the other in the face. She turned around and smacked that girls so hard on the side of the face you could have heard it all over the building. She never waited to be disqualified, she just piked for the dressing room. (Laughter)

You don't see anything of that kind today in girls' games, they are sportsmen.

There are one or two things I would like to change in the girls' rules. The first is I would do away with that holding of the ball for three seconds. There isn't any need for it. The girls are good sports and they can play. We have girls who can play just about as good basketball as the men. These Commercial Grads play with the University of Alberta, play with the boys and give them a good game.

That is one thing I would do away with. The second thing is that I would divide the court into two parts. I believe that is a good thing to prevent this running up and down. But in the second half of the game, I would have those playing forward in the first half changed to guards. If I had a girl playing basketball under the present rules she wouldn't play guard because she is an obstructionist, she doesn't get a chance to use initiative, but she does get all the chance in the world to be obstructionist and keep the other party back. We don't want to develop that type of individual and I say let the guards have a chance to play forward, let the forwards have a chance to play guard. With those two changes in the girls' rules, I believe that it would make the game ideally conditioned for the players, maybe not for the spectators, but it can be carried out. (Applause)

CHAIRMAN CAULKINS: I know there are going to be a lot of questions. We can't let this man go yet. Now for the questions. Don't be afraid and ask this man who is so full of information about this game which is his own child of forty years ago. Don't be afraid to ask questions on girls' rules or whatever it may be. Let's have about ten minutes of it.

Maybe the problems of the basketball are so hot nobody dares make himself so conspicuous by getting up and asking a question. But I am sure there are some.

QUESTION: I would like to know how the dribble originated.

DR. NAISMITH: The dribble originated in this way: When a player was facing the corner, for instance, and the other men were covered, it was a man to man game at the time; and the player was right behind him, so there wasn't any chance for him to get rid of that ball. What he did was roll it across the floor and then run after it. Theoretically, we are not permitted to move with the ball in our possession. When I roll it, theoretically I let it out of my possession, but I follow it as closely as I can and get it.

Then they began to bounce the ball, one bounce, and from one bounce they began to get a number of them. The dribble I consider one of the finest plays, one of the sweetest, prettiest plays in the whole bunch, and when they thought a few years ago of eliminating the dribble, I fought it as hard as I could.

QUESTION: Doctor, is there any way of stopping this whistle blowing, slowing up the game, that you have thought of?

DR. NAISMITH: Yes. If you allow it to become a little rough.

QUESTION: I mean to speed the game up, rather than having so many breaks in the game, breaking up the continuity of the play.

DR. NAISMITH: I don't know just exactly how you would meet that situation here. We don't have many of those. If you are thinking of the professional game, that is true, that whenever the ball went up against the cage, the whistle was blown to throw the ball up. I think that some persons become a little bit too technical in officiating along that line. Is that what you mean?

QUESTION: Yes, I mean to keep the game going.

DR. NAISMITH: How much faster do you want it? That is the criticism that we had, that the game is too fast. Personally, I would like to call the held ball pretty quickly, but not before the two individuals meet. I have seen that held ball called when the two individuals were coming together; the whistle was blown, and I don't think that is right. There ought to be a real held ball before the whistle is blown. If there is any roughness, you can call a foul on it.

There is a rule that I think would help matters considerably in that very way that has been eliminated, and that is there was one rule saying the ball can be held by the hands only; it is a foul to hold the ball with any other part of the body. I have seen boys in the middle of the floor dive at it and pull the ball right in to them, a held ball. So that there are a few factors there that might be helped. I think that rule might well be enforced. It might help that. Does that cover the ground, or is there any other phase of it now that I can bring out?

QUESTION: What do you think about this freezing the ball in the last few minutes when the team is ahead?

DR. NAISMITH: There isn't any such thing.

QUESTION: There isn't? They are doing it.

DR. NAISMITH: I don't care where the ball is, I have a right to go and get it, haven't I? Then you can't freeze it from me. There is where the whole trouble has come in. We blame the man who has the ball for holding it. I am not going to throw the ball away unless I have to. Come and get it. That is what I say, and that is what I have been fighting the rules committee on. They should make it plain that it is the duty of the persons, other than those who have the ball, to go and get it. Then you can't freeze them out. But the crowd is always against the fellow that has the ball. They say, "Why don't you go ahead?"

QUESTION: In a girls' game I recently observed, they counted a goal that was put in right under the basket with one hand [as] a one point shot. Is that the official ruling?

DR. NAISMITH: I think that ought to be abolished; that would be my opinion. Whenever a goal is made, let it count no matter how it is made. That is put in because of the other rule of holding the ball for three seconds. If you eliminate that, you eliminate this also. That is why I am in favor of doing away with that restriction at that point. It clears a lot of these things up and makes the game simpler. I do believe firmly that girls' teams ought to be coached by girls, not by boys. That is one of the handicaps that we have in our high schools where the boys coach the girls.

QUESTION: I would like to know if you use the three-division floor in Kansas.

DR. NAISMITH: We are getting away from it as far as we can. We use the two-division unless the floor is very large. We play crosswise of the court for the girls' game and just divide the court in two.

QUESTION: Was the center jump part of the game as originally played, or was it developed later?

DR. NAISMITH: The center jump was the first thing. I asked Duncan Patton to be one man and Frank Mahan was the other, and we threw the ball up between them, but it was thrown from outside bounds. It was thrown up between the two center men, yes, and there has been a great deal of criticism of that and there is one suggestion that I have made that I think would help and that is that the official throw the ball at varying heights. But as it is he throws it just a few inches above where the tallest man can reach, and he knows how to do it. I have stepped in and thrown the ball up and this fellow would stand frozen. It adds another factor, the factor of physical judgment. He has to wait until he can jump and touch that ball and it gives the shorter man an advantage in that way.

QUESTION: During the development of the game, has any consideration been given to the elementary boys as regards lowering the basket and using the smaller ball?

DR. NAISMITH: It has been considered, and so far there have been back stops made that could be raised and lowered. I think you will find those advertised in some places. Personally, I don't think it makes very much difference. I don't think it would do any harm to lower it. If as the boy grows up, the basket goes up, then he has gotten his reflexes working for that height. At the present time, we have boys in the elementary school that can throw goals just as well as some of the bigger fellows, some of the older fellows. It might be a good thing, but it would cause variation.

There has been an attempt to raise the goal two feet, and I have objected to that, because of that very fact that it would necessitate this thing if it were higher and also in the case of the Japanese and the Chinese who are short individuals; it would probably make them vary their goals also.

QUESTION: I don't think the rule book is very clear on the personal fouls. Can you explain that? I don't think it is absolutely clear.

DR. NAISMITH: I can't remember just exactly what you are thinking of there, but any foul against the person or the individual is a personal foul. A foul committed with the ball may be a technical violation. The violation has no penalty. A technical foul has a penalty.

QUESTION: I mean as far as actual body contact is concerned, when would it be a foul and when wouldn't it be?

DR. NAISMITH: I think the most flagrant case is where the man is dribbling the ball down the field and he comes in personal contact with the individual. Unless the guard has really made an advance and comes forward, I would call it on the dribbler every time. Why? Because the dribbler is using this particular method to [obtain] unfair advantage for himself. He is not supposed to do that. A dribble is not for the purpose of playing the game, but simply to be used under certain conditions. When two fellows come together and neither one is rougher than the other, what can you do? You can either call two fouls or let it go. I prefer to let it go, unless there is a deliberate intent. As far as I can see, you have got to depend a little bit on your interpretation there.

QUESTION: Would you call it charging?

DR. NAISMITH: Charging can be on either person, a dribbler charges when he comes in. The other man may come in and charge. If I stand there and he runs into me, I am not charging. I have a right to my position on the floor. He has no right to overrun me. He has no right to the position which I occupy. If he is going to knock me down and I throw my shoulder forward there and run into his chest, that is bad luck. That is where I say the one who is trying to get advantage by running is the one who is responsible for the contact. (Applause)

CHAIRMAN CAULKINS: I am sure it isn't necessary for me to make any additional speech to show Dr. Naismith we very much appreciate what he has done for us here this morning.

Just before introducing the next speaker, I want to say a word about the program for January and succeeding months. Let me impress, first of all, that the next session of this class will be on January 9. That is three weeks from today. As to the location and the subject and the program for the lectures of January, you will receive word by mail about the second of January. We are working up a program and it is not quite ready to announce, but it is going to be very interesting. We are going to take up baseball and swimming, some of the ice sports in January, track and field, and the other activities in the athletic program.

As I said in the beginning, in addition to having this discussion by a man who is an authority on the game of basketball as played every where, we want to bring the game down to home conditions. So George Barclay of the Newtown High School, coach of the team there, is here with his players and will have the rest of the session to discuss his system of coaching basketball in a New York City high school and to give us a demonstration following it. (Applause)

MR. GEORGE BARCLAY: I feel like a fellow in the kindergarten after following Dr. Naismith, the master of the development and technic and coaching of the game. However, having coached in the high schools here in the city for a few years, I was asked to outline the procedure that I follow from the time I give my first call to the time we play our last game.

The first thing that I was asked to bring up is methods and means of getting candidates out. I have found from experience that the best place to issue the call for candidates is in the gymnasium; second, in your study halls. By all means if you have a weekly publication in your school, have it issued there. These notices should be posted on all the bulletin boards so each and every boy student can see and know about the call for practice. These notices should be posted at least one week before the first practice session.

The first practice session when the candidates appear (of course, I am taking the numbers that I am dealing with) my call for basketball candidates usually brings out anywhere from 135 [to 285] candidates for the team. Some schools may not have such a large group to work with. But at the first call, the first thing that is mentioned is scholarship, and in scholarship the rules of the P. S. A. L. of New York City state to be eligible to play basketball, or any sport, a boy must be successfully carrying three prepareds and one unprepared subject.

At once I state that if I have the perpetual flunker before me, I would a good deal rather have him withdraw himself at the close of that day. I do not care to waste time on fellows who are going to fail out at the mid-term or the final marking periods.

The next point of importance to bring up is regarding the care and cleanliness of the individual. We all know that basketball is a game that produces a great deal of perspiration, especially if you work your boys hard and teach them basketball. You have to instruct them then in soaping down and washing thoroughly to prevent boils and abscesses and so forth.

Another frequent occurrence in the matter of injuries is the floor burn and the blister. If you can convince your students in front of you that it is much easier to take care of these injuries at the first sign of them, there will be very few infections and you will not lose many of your players during the year due to infections.

Then I mention the fact that regular attendance is not only desired, but absolutely insisted upon, and if any of the boys are working on the outside three afternoons a week, they cannot expect to make the varsity basketball team, and so I ask them to withdraw.

I was asked to mention diet. Unfortunately, in the high schools of New York City, the diet question does not concern us a great deal. We have not a training table for the boys as they have in colleges, but it is suggested to them that they eat wholesome meals, well-balanced meals; that they refrain from drinking coffee and tea and that milk and cocoa be taken instead. They are asked not to eat a great amount of chocolates and not to take the chocolate sundaes and other sodas and drinks.

Another thing that I absolutely insist upon is the matter of smoking. If any boy on my squad is seen smoking by me, no questions are asked; he is merely told to turn in his uniform. The matter of conditioning is very important, and, therefore, a boy to play good basketball must have good wind, and smoking and good wind do not go together.

In the first week, after the first meeting of the group, they are told to come in uniform and sneaks at the first session. At the practice session, the discussion is given regarding the various types of passes. We have the general straight over arm pass, either right or left, the underhand pass, single or double; the bounce pass and the hook pass. The boys will demonstrate these various passes later on in the day.

After instructing them in these passes, having the veterans of the previous year's team demonstrate the passes, I divide the group into six divisions, sending one division to each basket, placing each division in charge of a veteran of the previous year. I myself take a position on the platform and watch the procedure from that point. I have instructed the veterans that if they see any boy with exceptional ability in handling the ball or in scoring, to at once come to me and call my attention to that boy so I can watch him. This system has been very satisfactory, and I recommend it.

It reminds me of a case brought to my attention last year. One of the high schools here in New York, a very strong high school in basketball, gave their call for candidates. The coach appeared and gave a talk. The first two practice sessions he merely went out onto the floor and left the squad in charge of his veterans of the previous year. On the fifth day of practice he posted a list, retaining twenty-two members. On this list was omitted the name of a fellow that if I used his name at the present time, many of you would know. He was an outstanding basketball player in the Church House League for the last three seasons. He has never played on his high school team, merely because he was not in a certain clique of this particular school. That is one thing. When I mention the word, "clique," do not let cliques or fraternities govern your team. Nothing can break down the morale of a prospective basketball player quicker than to feel that he has to be in with a certain gang, belong to a certain club or something to make the team.

After the week of watching them handle the ball and passing in the drilling, we divide the group at each basket, as I stated, into two lines. We have them pass to the other line and shoot, pass, receive and shoot, pass, dribble and lay up. Those are the activities we take in these line formations.

Then for the second and third weeks, I divide the entire squad into teams. We have scrimmages, because I feel the best place to see a boy's ability is in scrimmage. The teams stay together for the next two weeks, but if I notice that in making the teams a boy who would be classified in one group on height or weight is an exceptional basketball player and is out of place in that group that he has been assigned to, I at once find one in the group that is further along and interchange the players to equalize the competition because in that way you are able to detect fellows who can play basketball in equalized competition. It is unfair to expect that putting your varsity players against your second termers you are going to have a basketball game, because you are not.

On the other hand, if you try to equalize, keep your second termers together, if you have an exceptional player in your second term, bring him up and put him in with a higher term where he will meet boys of equal caliber and ability.

At the end of the third week, I cut my squad from 135 or whatever it is, down to approximately 55 or 60. I reorganize the teams and after reorganizing the teams, we play once more for a period of three weeks, and during these scrimmages, the scrimmages are stopped and corrections are made, various discussions are brought about regarding tips and forms, positions on the floor and so forth.

At the end of the sixth week, I make my final cut of the season, keeping 35 fellows in uniform for the remainder of the year. The first squad consists of 15 and the remaining 20 are on the second squad.

Naturally, some may feel that I am unjust in this stand, but on my second squad I have no one that is above a six termer for the simple reason you are working to develop in the second squad prospective varsity players, although you may be depriving the seventh and eighth-termer of an opportunity to play on your second team, with the object of getting the younger boys playing the game and in hopes of having a boy develop into varsity timber.

I am cutting down some of the things because of the time, so the next thing I will mention is the types of offense.

As we know, basketball's main object is to score baskets, two points for the basket from the floor and one point if you successfully make the attempt from the foul line. Therefore, there have been various types of offenses that have been generally accepted. The first type, and probably the one used by the majority of schools, is the straight five-man offense, every man weaving in and out, trying to get in scoring position and receiving a pass from a team mate to lay the ball up and score the basket.

Another type is the four-and-one offense, four men weaving and interweaving, cutting, cutting, at all times waiting for the opening for the pass, and one man in the defense position ready to cover any player of the opposition that happens to break loose on the recovery of the ball by his team mate.

Then we have the offense of the three and two, three men offense, two men defense, usually used by teams that are playing a defensive game, that are endeavoring to hold the opposition score down, and that type will be demonstrated, as all these types will be, in the scrimmage and the play that follows.

Then we have an offense. I don't know of anyone else that uses it. It is a three, one and one. You will see it out here today. It is an offense where I have one man in the safety defense position, in the vicinity of the foul circle, one man about center, and three men alternating into the corners, waiting for passes and an opening to lay the ball up in scoring position.

I was going to give you set formation of offensive play. I might just mention them here and have the boys run through them on the court. Of course, the first play is a very simple play, the forward cross. The center tips the ball either to his right or left. The forward accepts it, makes a pass to his opposite forward underneath the basket. It is a play that is very easily broken up, if you have instructed your guards to merely shift into the center of the play and intercept the forward cross play.

The second play in set formation is a forward to center. Tap the ball to the forward; center goes around his man, cuts to the foul line, receives a return pass from the forward that he tapped the ball to and either lays it up or gives it to the other forward who is cut into the opposite zone.

There you have the play of the forward to center to guard. This play is very effective for the simple reason that as the opposing guard comes in to cover your center, after he comes down in [the lane,] after tapping the ball to the forward, he leaves an opening for your guard to go around. Your guard swings right around, receives a pass from the center, usually an underhand hook or bounce pass and lays the ball up.

Then the other play in offensive basketball that has been very successful is a straight guard around, where the ball is tapped to the forward and the forward lays the ball over his head to a guard who has circled back of him.

Now as to defensive basketball. Some coaches say that your defense is merely as strong as your offense. But I like to build up a very strong defense. If you have a defensive team and a forward and a center can score a few points for you, you are very apt to win a lot of the ball games.

In picking my guards, in the group of over 100 fellows, I usually have some pretty big boys. These fellows are chosen; and today you will see two boys, both third termers, one is six feet two and weighs 202 pounds. I expect a great deal of him. The other is five feet eleven and weighs 182 pounds. So something will come from those boys, I am sure.

There are four types of defense that the boys are coached in. Of course, some of you know the Newtown team (this talk here this morning was supposed to be for those who are just starting the coaching game, but I see quite a number of my worthy colleagues here and fellows who probably know a lot more about basketball than I do).

Of the four types of defense the Newtown team uses, the one that you all expect me to mention first is the zone defense, three to two. You will see it out here this morning, two men in the back court, three men across the front. The reason that I like the zone defense, the five-man zone, is the fact that in high school basketball you are dealing with the adolescent boy. If your team has got ahead, why insist on a straight man to man defense, having them run themselves to death? You have got the lead, drop back into your defense position and your boys while they are waiting for your opponents to start an offense are resting. When your team gains possession of the ball, you have got two forwards ready to cut fast and with two guards in the center to feed them, you are very [apt] to break away from a four-man offense or a five-man offense [and] have two men going down the court clear. That is the reason that I prefer the five-man defense. Of course, some of you were here two years ago when Nat Holman spoke, when the question was asked him by one of the coaches of Queens, how to beat a five-man zone defense, you will remember he said the five-man zone defense was a dandy defense and the only way to beat it was to get the lead and make them break the defense. That is the idea; get the lead. That is the first important thing. You get the lead, then the boys will have to go out and play man to man and from painful experience I have learned that I had to instruct the boys in man to man defense and now they know it.

The second defense is straight man to man, or in the terms of the basketball player, dogging the man, chasing the man all around. The rules of basketball state you are not supposed to play the man, but I defy any of you to go into any high school or college game and see the players watching the ball consistently; as you see a forward cut, you will see the guard watch the forward. He is not watching where the ball is coming from; he is watching what position that forward is going to get into. So although this is in the rules, I am afraid there would be a great deal of whistle blowing if we interpreted literally the fact that you are supposed to play the ball and not the men.

Then another defense is the four and one defense that is used by Springfield College quite consistently. It is otherwise known as a volley ball defense. You have four men in a zone, two men in the rear, two men in front and one man roaming around in the forward court, hoping to intercept the starting formations of an offense by the opponents. At times it works very nicely, at other times the fellow has faded out of position and lo and behold there is a perfect break for the basket and unless you have good defense, usually the way they work it, they cut down in the center of the court and as they bring your two guards in to cover the center play, a quick pass is given to the corner and then a hook pass is crossed back under the basket and it is very simple defense to beat.

I mentioned before, the three, one and one offense. The reason I use this three, one and one offense is because it is also a defense position. You will see the team this morning use that, and you can judge of its value in the scrimmage.

That completes the three offenses and the four defenses that I wanted to give you.

Now a few hints to forwards and a few hints to guards and I will get the boys out and let them do the rest.

Hints to forwards. First, never shoot when off balance. Second, remember that basketball is a team game, therefore, do not get [arm] weary throwing them up. Third, when two men cut for the basket play and you break into a fast offense and your two forwards are cutting for the basket, don't be afraid to use the one-two. The one-two, as you probably know, is to receive and give back to the man who gave you the pass. Don't be afraid to return the pass. Fourth, watch closely your opportunities for pivot plays.

In professional basketball, they have eliminated the pivot. In high school basketball and elementary school basketball, the pivot is still permitted. I mention the pivot play here. I do not mean the pivot play where one man places himself on the foul line or in the vicinity and receives a sharp pass out from a team mate holding it until you get an opening for your cut. The pivot play I refer to is when a forward receives a beautiful pass from a guard or center and makes a fast cut and a guard is in a position to stop the play; he stops and by glancing over his shoulder sees which way the guard is playing him and pivots in the opposite direction and either passes or lays it up.

The fifth, keep on your toes and cut, cut, cut. The forwards have got to keep moving. If your opposition are playing you man to man defense, let those guards run and run plenty.

Hints to guards: The first hint, and the thing I try to impress on my guards from the very beginning when I start with them as second termers is that they are fundamentally defensive players and therefore, the point they prevent is just as important to the team as the one that the forward center scores. The guard in basketball may be likened to the line man in football. There is not a great deal of publicity for the line man, but there is a great deal of work done by him.

The second point, be careful not to follow feints. Don't follow when a man shifts. He is going to return. If you follow, as I just explained, it gives the opening for the pivot play and a beautiful lay up. So instruct your guards not to follow shifts.

Also instruct them, as the third point, to keep their feet well apart and have a well balanced stance so they can start in either direction and be ready to intercept a play on either side of their particular position.

Then the next point, put it down in capital letters, for it is very important, especially to high schools: BE CAREFUL OF PER-SONAL FOULS. Naturally, personal fouls mean eviction from the game. You cannot have excessive fouling. Therefore, instruct how to go up to block a shot without coming in personal contact with your man; by going up straight, if there is a personal contact the forward charging into the guard, it is a foul on the forward, if it is called, and not on the guard, who is in [the air . . . he went up straight with his arms over knocking down the shot. Then another] very important thing is for a guard never to leave his feet. The only place he leaves his feet is under the back board when he is pulling the ball off. If he leaves his feet in the forward zones, it is just too bad because as the forward feints a shot and the guard goes up in the air, leaving his feet, the forward merely lowers his shoulders and dribbles around the guard and is in a beautiful scoring position.

There is one thing I mean to speak of in diet. I want to show you the problem of a high school coach in New York. This morning I have ten boys here. Four of them are Italians. I imagine they have their spaghetti and ravioli. Four of them are Irishmen. I imagine they have their corned beef and cabbage. The other two are Germans. I imagine they like their sauerkraut. So you can just see the problem of a high school coach in regard to diet.

. . . Mr. Barclay demonstrated the various plays with his teams from the Newton High School.

. . . The meeting adjourned at twelve o'clock.

1. Born in Canada, James Naismith earned degrees from McGill University and Presbyterian College in Montreal before becoming a physical education instructor at the International YMCA Training School in Springfield MA. Springfield College Archives and Special Collections.

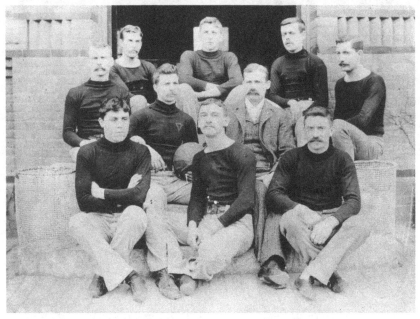

2. (top) While a student at McGill University, James Naismith invented the headgear players wore while participating in football. Naismith (*left*) is wearing the headgear while hiking the ball to a teammate. Kenneth Spencer Research Library, University of Kansas Libraries.

3. (bottom) James Naismith (*right, middle row*) sits with the first basketball team on the steps of the old gymnasium at the International YMCA Training School. Springfield College Archives and Special Collections.

4. James Naismith was a thirty-year-old physical education instructor when he was given the assignment to come up with a new game for a physical education class. Springfield College Archives and Special Collections.

5. (above) James Naismith (*standing top right*) was the first head coach of the Kansas basketball team. He is posing with the 1898–99 team. Kenneth Spencer Research Library, University of Kansas Libraries.

6. (opposite top) James Naismith (*center*) is next to Kansas head coach Phog Allen. The 1923 Kansas basketball team went 17-1 and was named national champions by the Helms Athletic Foundation. Kenneth Spencer Research Library, University of Kansas Libraries.

7. (opposite bottom) Later in life, James Naismith recreates the early origins of basketball as he tosses the ball into a peach basket. Kenneth Spencer Research Library, University of Kansas Libraries.

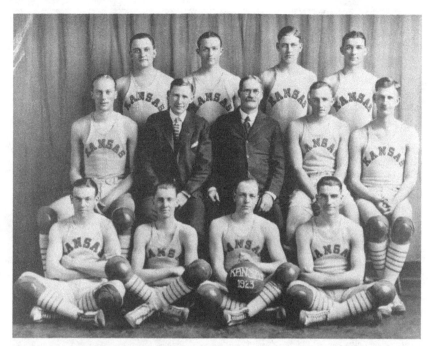

8. James Naismith (*left*) and Phog Allen (*right*) pose together holding a basketball. Kenneth Spencer Research Library, University of Kansas Libraries.

9. James Naismith poses with a leather basketball while on the faculty at the University of Kansas. Kenneth Spencer Research Library, University of Kansas Libraries.

10. James Naismith poses with a leather soccer ball and two peach baskets, which was reminiscent of the first game of basketball in December 1891. Kenneth Spencer Research Library, University of Kansas Libraries.

11. Later in his career, James Naismith became a well-regarded instructor and chaplain at the University of Kansas. In 1936 he traveled to the Berlin Olympics to watch basketball become an Olympic sport for the first time. Springfield College Archives and Special Collections.

12. Later in life, James Naismith often returned to Canada, his birthplace. This photo is on such a trip as he poses with his two dogs. Kenneth Spencer Research Library, University of Kansas Libraries.

The Origin of Basket Ball

January 5, 1932

A speech titled "The Origin of Basket Ball" given by James Naismith at Springfield College on January 5, 1932.

I have been asked to speak on the origin of basket ball and I feel a little embarrassed about this because it is more or less personal, but wherever I go no matter how fine a talk or lecture I may give, always two questions are asked of me either at the time or afterwards:

1. How did you come to think of it?
2. Has it changed much since that time?

These are two thoughts in the minds of people, out of curiosity, or from interest in the game itself. I am going to try to give you a full idea of basket ball, its origin and some of the changes that have taken place—very few in my limited time.

In order to get an idea of the origin of the game, it is necessary for us to know something of the situations in which we were at that time. I look at the young people coming into physical education today with all the facilities for work and with all the different games and sports; in fact, we have come to the point where a great deal of physical education is games and the policy of many institutions is games.

In 1890, when I first entered this institution there were practically no games with the exception of football, baseball and track; football in the fall, baseball and track in the spring. Soccer we played very little. From the time that we stopped playing football in the fall until baseball began in the spring, we had nothing but work on the horse, buck, and different pieces of apparatus, along with calisthenics. I wonder what men in physical education today would do with that limited sphere to work in; how would we get along? That was the condition we had and we all felt, Drs. Seerley, Clark, Gulick and Stagg, that we should get together and talk it over. We needed some sort of game that would be interesting and could be played indoors. We had three games: three-deep, line ball, and Dr. Gulick's game called cricket.

We had a seminar in which we discussed these things quite frequently. It was a seminar in psychology and one day in discussing inventions, Dr. Gulick made this statement: "There is nothing new under the sun, but all new things are simply a recombination of the factors of existing things." That was the proposition made to us. We simply re-combined the factors of the old and made the new.

After thinking it over, I said to Dr. Gulick: "If that is true, we can go to work and invest a new game." Nothing much more was said about it but Dr. Stagg said he assigned that as our home work for the next meeting but no one brought in any record at all.

There was a class of secretarial men, twenty to twenty-five years of age. Most of them played on the football team and when the winter season came and they were put on the parallel bars, etc. they had no interest in them. They did not care for it, they were not interested in learning it, and there was no fun in it. Dr. Clark, who is present today, one of the finest athletes and gymnasts we had in the institution, a graduate of Williams, a medical man, everything in the world that could make a man efficient in work of this kind, found that same condition. It was not individuals at all, but existing conditions.

At a faculty meeting Dr. Clark spoke and told how difficult it was to handle these men. He made another statement saying "The difficulty is, with that particular group of men what we want is recreative work; something that will please them and something they will want to do."

I told Dr. Clark that if he would play games, he would get the attention of those fellows. After a little while, Dr. Gulick said "Naismith, I wish you would take charge of that class." If I ever tried to back out of anything, I did then. I did not want to do it. I had charge of a group interested in boxing, wrestling, fencing and swimming and I was perfectly satisfied with my work. Dr. Gulick said he wanted me to do it. I had to do it or get out and I felt pretty sore about it. I thought Dr. Gulick had imposed on me by giving me something I did not want to do and compelling me to do it. As we walked along the hall, talking about it, he said "Naismith, this would be a good time for you to invent that new game you said you could." I closed my fist, and looked at Dr. Gulick's face for a spot to plant my fist, but I saw a peculiar twinkle in his eye which seemed to say "put up or shut up".

He then said I could do two things: 1. I could make up a game. 2. The game must interest that group.

Whether or not he realized the importance of what he did at that time I don't know but it turned out to be the best thing that could have been done.

I took that class—not in very good humor, nor grace. We tried to play football indoors, but broke the arms and legs of the players. It proved to be too rough, and it was not long before the boys rebelled against it. We then tried soccer, but broke all the windows. Then we tried lacrosse and broke up the apparatus. We found that this did not work.

I sat at my desk one day, scratching my head, trying to work something out. This thought came to me: They all liked to play football. Why can't we play it indoors?—Because it is too rough. Why is it rough?—Because we tackle. Why do we tackle?—Because we run with the ball. If we did not run with the ball, there would be no necessity for tackling. We need a game to play indoors.——I had it! Just by asking myself these few questions—Why? I think that is one of the biggest things in the world today.

(We have developed into two classes: Scientist who inquire How. Philosophers who inquire Why. The philosophers are so few we do not get very far. If the scientists told us how and then why, we would be a good deal better off in the world—this is only on the side, away from the origin of basket ball.)

If we don't let them run with the ball, what are we going to do? Think of a goal of some kind. In soccer, and lacrosse, we had a perpendicular goal and a goal keeper, but this difficulty with that was that in order to make a goal you had to throw the ball with as much speed as possible. The harder you threw, the more chance there was for you to make a goal. That again made for roughness. I thought of the underhand swing. That is a negative rule and negative rules do not work efficiently.

I was stumped for a while. By and by I began to think of a little game I had played near Affleck's home—Duck on the Rock. We found a rock two feet high and two feet across. Each one took a stone about the size of his fist. One put his stone on the rock and the rest of us got behind a line and tried to knock it off. We would throw our stones as hard as we could at his and if we happened to hit it, it was all right, but if we missed it, we went way down. Once in a while we threw the ball in such a way that it would knock his off and come back again and we would walk up and get it.

I think I have it! Instead of throwing the ball straight for the goal, let us throw it in a curve and we cannot throw it hard. You must take your time and use skill instead of power and speed. Then I thought of putting a mark on the floor; just a circle, and use that for the goal, but the goal keeper would stand in it and we could not make the goal. Put it above his head and no one can stand in it and you would have a chance of making a goal once in a while. It would be horizontal and high in the air.

My next thought was how was I going to put it in play? I used Gulick's idea of taking parts of other games. Polo—put the ball in the center, line the team up at both ends and have them rush for the ball. There would be a mix-up in the center of the floor when that happened so that idea was thrown out. I recalled in playing English Rugby that when the ball goes out of bounds, two forward lines line up at right angles to the side line where the ball goes out; the umpire stands outside, back of the line, and throws the ball in between the two lines. But I remembered that when we jumped for the ball the elbows interfered and there was much roughness. If we took two men out of that group and put them in the center, there would be no roughness. I did not appreciate the ingenuity of American boys for I have seen some pretty rough things done. We threw it from the outside in on the floor. Then I thought that the ball must be thrown in such a way as to fall between the two center players.

We went to work and jotted down some of these thoughts. There were thirteen of them—until that time thirteen was an unlucky number for me but since then it has changed. I had these typed and carried them down and pinned them up on the bulletin board. As I was going down with a soccer ball in my hand, as I had concluded we would want a round light ball, I met "Pop" Stebbins. I said, "Have you got a couple of boxes eighteen inches square?" He said, "No, but I have a couple of old peach baskets." He brought them up and I nailed one at each end of the gallery—ten feet from the floor. If the gallery had been eleven feet high the goals would probably have been at that height today.

I got things ready and the class came down. Frank Mahan, a big, burly Irishman who played tackle on the football team, came down among the first and my mind was pretty well disturbed. I had a soccer ball in my hand, two peach baskets on the wall and an idea in my head. I did not know how to go about it. My future as I looked at it then depended on the throw of the ball. When Mahan came down he looked up and saw one basket, then he looked around and saw another one. "Humpf" he said "another new game." That was the attitude they all had and they were ready to scrap anything brought before them. They did not want to give in to me but I called them up. There were eighteen men in the class. I divided it into two sections, nine men on a side at first. Mahan was center on one side, Patton on the other. I tossed the ball between them and I never had any more trouble with the class, or the game. The class took to it and the only difficulty I had was to drive them out when the hour closed.

Another reason was: There was a school not very far away. Our gymnasium was down in the basement and the door opened on to the street. A number of school teachers used to come in and watch the boys play games and added incentive to playing. The regular hour was between 11 and 12. At the close of that hour every day the girls would come in and the boys would play ball for them. Soon there were as many as 100 people watching the game from the gallery. It was not long until some of the teachers came to me and asked why they could not play the game. I did not see any reason why they could not. I thought it was a good game and would be all right for them.

After consultation they were given a certain hour to practice. You boys don't know what clothes the girls wore then—bustles, hoops and high heels—and they played in them! It was not long until the stenographers of the school got up another team. Some of us young unmarried men got our sweethearts interested in it and we got a ladies faculty team. The girls asked me to umpire. I agreed to but I didn't know as much about ladies as I do now. We got along nicely until I called a foul on one of the girls. She asked, "Did you call a foul on me?" and then she told me where I came from, where I was going to, and what my character was! I tried to pacify her but couldn't do it. The only way was to toss up the ball and then she had to fall into her place.

That girl was not different from other girls. They never had a chance to take part in any game where sportsmanship was required. It was something new for them. Some had played shuttle cock and a few other games similar to that; they had not even played tennis. For a number of years the rules were adopted as unsportsmanlike conduct among women. This is not true today. Some of the finest sportsmanship has been exhibited in women's basket ball games. They never had the chance to do that sort of thing and get into the line of sportsmanship. I felt if basket ball did not do anything else than relieve womankind from that condition, it was well worth putting into existence.

Basketball has been played on roller skates, on horseback, and in the water so the game has been extended from that time.

Since coming to this institution there are two things that struck me:

1. As I stood in the gallery the other day and watched the class of one hundred men on the floor, I thought back to 1891 when there were three men in the physical department: Harvey Smith, Myron Rideout, and Webb.
2. Another thing was that the boys seemed to be very uniform in size. There used to be stubby men and tall men. I was try-

ing to find the tall men but I could not. Why is this? I made this remark to Mr. Brock. His reply was, "We select our men." What a difference in 1891! We used to go out and compel them to come in and now some of them are compelled to stay out. What a wonderful change in forty years!

This thought came to me—why do we have so many now in comparison with that time? It was a very different proposition going into physical education work in 1890 than it is now. When I decided to enter physical work and spoke to a young man whom I expected to be my brother-in-law, he asked "What are you going to do now?" I replied, "I am going to Springfield and take up athletics." Then he said, "Athletics to the devil." When I first played football on the McGill team in 1883 a group of my chums got together and had a prayer meeting over me because I was playing on the varsity team. You would not realize that now but it is a fact. The change of attitude is illustrated in a letter which I received from the man who started that prayer meeting. He wrote, "In thinking over our old class I don't think any one has made a bigger contribution to the building of character than the one who invented basket ball." There is a difference in outlook on physical education today from what it was at that time. Men had to enter that work against the general opinion and they had to have more or less of a missionary spirit in working out their ideas of what good could be done.

I hope you will pardon a personal experience, but it may help you. Way back in my college days I was lying on the bed one Sunday and thought: What is this all about? What is life about? What are you going to do? What are you going to be? What motto will you hold up before you? I put up on the wall, not in writing, but in my mind this thought: "I want to leave the world a little bit better than I found it." That is the motto I had then and it is the motto I have today. That has been a mighty fine thing to me.

I was studying theology and planning to be a minister as that looked to be the best thing I could do. During football practice when McNutt was playing guard, something went wrong. The air went blue with profanity. In the northern woods we have nothing else to do but practice profanity and he was a good exponent of it. By and by he turned around to me and said, "I beg your pardon. I forgot you were there." I had heard worse than that before but I thought: why should anyone apologize to me for profanity? I went to Dr. Budge, secretary of the Y M C A, and told him "I believe that there was something in playing the game square, playing it hard with all the intensity that you have, but playing it square. I think you can influence men by doing that sort of thing." Dr. Budge told me they had a school for that very thing in Springfield, and I told him I was going to see it.

I came in the summer and saw what you were doing. I took a trip not only in this state but out through the west to see how Y M C A's worked, and found that there was a possibility of building and developing the character of the individual through physical activities. I have never regretted it. I asked my sister and uncle a few years ago if they had forgiven me for not becoming a minister. They shook their heads. I had gone against their wishes but I am not sorry and I have found it is a tremendously fine thing for the building of character.

The best definition of character I know is: It is that combination of reflexes within me which determine how I shall act under unforeseen circumstances. The reflexes you build on the floor are going to become a part of your character. The best illustration of that is:

An old watchman was riding a horse through the main street close to the university just as the students were going out. His hat blew off and he couldn't very well get off the horse. I wondered what the students would do to this old man. How would they react to the situation? Two boys ran out from opposite sides of the street and one of them got the hat and returned it to the owner. Those two boys were brothers, brought up in the same home, athletes of the finest type, track and football men. I thought what an opportunity there is for men in physical education to develop those characters that will live with them through life.

That is what we are after. It is not the money we are going to get out of it. I had a man write me thirty years after saying: "I have just been thinking over things and I am mighty glad I knew you." I did not know I had any influence on him. It is your inner life, the things you do and say that will influence those fellows and make them men. I wish every one of you boys the pleasure not only of having a successful football team, but of having a bunch of fellows come up and say, "I am glad I knew you. You have been a help in my life."

Radio Interview

—

1932

A radio interview conducted of James Naismith on December 15, 1932, in which he discusses the game's history and eventual spread.

1. Surely good Canadian weather isn't it Doctor—Fellow will have to watch his ears tonight. Say I was just wondering—What was your first position in physical education?

    ANSWER: My first position as a physical educator was in McGill University, Montreal, Canada.

2. How long ago was that and how did you happen to take it up?

    ANSWER: That was in the fall of 1887. I had graduated from the University that spring, and had entered the seminary for a three-year course. During the summer, Mr. Barnjum, who had been our gymnastic instructor, died; leaving a vacancy in that department. I had been a leader in his group and made application for the position and secured it.

3. Did you take part in any collegiate athletics as well as in gymnastics?

    ANSWER: Yes. I played on the varsity football team for 6 years; three while in the University, and three while in the seminary. There were no restrictions at that time as to the number of years a player could compete, nor as to whether he had graduated but was still in connection with university.

4. How could you take part in athletics and also take charge of gymnastics? Did they not conflict after a time?

    ANSWER: They did not conflict. We practiced football from six to seven in the morning as that was the only time in which the medical students could practice. My work in the gymnasium came from five in the afternoon until ten p.m.

5. Did this amount of outside work not interfere with your scholastic standing?

ANSWER: It may have interfered somewhat, as I graduated only second in my class in both the ordinary and honor work; securing the Knox Silver Medal and the Crescent Scholarship for proficiency in both of these courses.

6. How could this be accomplished doing both physical work and scholastic?

ANSWER: Well I suppose it was simply by using the same intense drive in my studies that I used on the football field or in the gymnasium; making the brain work as hard in a scholastic field as the brawn and reflexes worked in the athletic.

7. I understand that you graduated from a theological seminary and was prepared to be a preacher. How did you happen to switch to physical education?

ANSWER: The reason of my transfer was because I felt that there was a new field in which could be done for mankind as well as in preaching and that some people could be able to do better work in one field than the other. Athletics and gymnastics at that time were looked on as the advice of the Devil to lead young men astray, however, I felt that if the Devil was making use of them to lead young men, it must have some natural attraction, and that they might be used to lead to a good end as well as to a bad one. The incident that led me to a serious consideration of this matter was one that occurred on the football field.

My position on the team was center, the guard next to me, when something went wrong, became very fluent in profanity. When he cooled down a little he turned to me and said, "I beg your pardon Jim, I forgot you were there". I had never said anything to him about profanity, nor even winced when he used that kind of language—all my life in the lumber camps, and had several experiences of a like nature. I began to wonder what it was that led men to do this for I never was considered a goody-goody boy or even stude but took my knocks in life or in athletics with a grin. I talked the matter with the Young Men's Christian Association secretary who told me about the Springfield Training School. I made up my mind that if my abilities lay along that line, I should use them; and when I graduated from the seminary, I went to Springfield. There I met Staag who had come to Yale with very much the same idea and also Black and Bond from Knox.

8. You have played both English and American Football. Is it true that the American game was an outgrowth of English Rugby?

ANSWER: Yes I feel quite sure that American Football is simply a modification of English Rugby. The American colleges began to play English Rugby it being introduced by some of the students from England who came to Harvard University. Harvard invited McGill to come down and play a game in the late seventies. Everything went on nicely as both teams were playing the same kind of football. A few years later, McGill which had stuck to the English game again came to Cambridge to play with Harvard, but the American game had been changed to such that they played one day with the English rules and the next day with the American. The main difference between English Rugby and American Football was that in the American game one side was given complete control of the ball in the scrimmage; while in the English game, the ball was rolled in by the referee and either team had an equal chance to secure it. A second change came in the fact that in the American game; players were permitted with the man who had the ball; while in the English game this was prohibited. The later changes have come in order to meet these changing conditions.

9. How does our game today differ from football as you played it?

ANSWER: In the nineties the watchword was to send the greatest power possible against the weakest point in the opponents line. This led to amassing of the offense and finally resulted in the wedge game; in which eleven men with their arms linked together made an attack on the weakest part of the opponent's line. When the opponents learned to stop the wedge, one man was sent through the opening in the line who had a large leather belt with a loop which the player with the ball could seize, and with two or three men pushing behind endeavor to make their five yards in three downs. This, of course, was varied with end runs and an occasional punt. In 1906, Staag suggested the elimination of the pushing and pulling of the man with the ball, and this has compelled the player with the ball to get his own momentum. The next radical change was when the forward pass was introduced; thus opening up the defense so that the single runner would have a better chance to make gains through the line. These have changed the game from one of power to one of skill and finesse.

10. In your judgment, how do the football players of today differ from those in your day?

ANSWER: The football players of the nineties were mostly developed by hard work and hard knocks. At that time all kinds of work was done mainly by the hands; today most of it is done by machinery—even the farm boy today rides the plow and the cultivator, binding and shocking of wheat is eliminated by the header or the combine. The hayfork has taken the place of the hand-fork, and the circular saw, the place of the axe and the buck-saw. Under these conditions how is it possible for the youth of today to get the power and the vigor that was obtained in the earlier days? The football players today, learn to dodge by stepping in boxes. In the early days he learned to dodge the charge of an angry bull or the heel of a fractious horse. He had to tackle a horse that refused to be caught; or any one of the animals on the farm. Anyone who is accustomed to bull-dogging a steer could easily learn to tackle a runner and throw him. The capacities of the student today are the same as they were then, but the opportunities for development are not present or are neglected.

11. Have you a continuous file of the basket ball rules?

ANSWER: I have in my possession, the first copy of the basket ball rules which is a vest pocket edition, and a copy of each succeeding year up to the present time with the exception of about three years.

12. Into how many different languages have the rules been translated?

ANSWER: I could not answer this definitely, but I do know and I have in my possession copies of the translation in French, Scheck, Greek, Japanese, Chinese, and Turkish. Last summer I received a notice that they were translating the rules in South America into Spanish and Portuguese. There may be others, but I have no knowledge of them.

13. I understand that you took up athletics before you took up gymnastics. Why did you take up the latter?

ANSWER: In my sophomore in the university, two young men; one a junior and the other a senior; one an athlete and the other an invalid came into my room one evening and told me that if I did not take some form of active exercise I was in danger of losing my health and failing in my work. They told me about the gymnasium and the opportunities that it provided for the care of my health. I felt perfectly healthy and perfectly strong and saw no need for any activity to keep me in good condition, but I realized that their experience was probably better than any that I had and that it was my obligation to accept their statement. Very shortly afterwards I made my way down to the University Gymnasium and soon became a regular attendant; finding that it kept me in excellent health. I soon became interested in the work and followed it up faithfully during the rest of my time in the University.

14. What college was the first to take up basket ball?

ANSWER: Of course Springfield was the first as it originated in that institution, so far as I have been able to find out, is either Geneva or the University of Iowa. In the letter from Dr. Callenburg, who was physical director in the University of Iowa, from 1891 for several years, he states that in the fall of 1892 he introduced the game into that institution. During the summer months, he visited a number of the Indian reservations, in each of which they set up a pair of goals made of wooden hoops and the Indians played the game with a great deal of enthusiasm and became quite proficient. In 1893, Mrs. Carver of Greensville, Texas wrote me; asking for a copy of the rules. In 1893, W. O. Black carried it to Leland Stanford where both boys and girls took up the game and competed the University of California.

Letter to Mr. R. G. Roberts

January 23, 1937

Letter written by James Naismith to Mr. R. G. Roberts on January 23, 1937, in which he discusses the uniforms from the early years of the game.

University of Kansas
Lawrence.

Division of Physical Education
and
Intercollegiate Athletics

1. / 23./ 37.

Mr R. G. Roberts
105 East 22nd St
New York City. N.Y.

My dear Roberts:-

I do not happen to have a picture of myself in our uniform except a large one and that is not in good shape.

My uniform on the day of the first game was the regular gymnastic uniform at that time. Grey trousers with a black stripe down the side, a black sleeveless jersey with a three inch triangle. The black elksole shoes, and black belt.

I have been asked several times to put on a replica of that first game, but it is very difficult to do so. What I have asked is 18 men who have never seen a game of basketball or heard about it.

I have worn a mustache since I was 20 years of age and the style at that time was what is now known as a walrus mustache.

There are several pictures of myself at that time but not in uniform of the gymnasium.

Wishing you every success, and kindest remembrances to Ned Irish I am

Most sincerely yours
James Naismith

Basketball—a Game the World Plays

The Rotarian, *January 1939*

An article James Naismith wrote entitled "Basketball—a Game the World Plays" that was published in January 1939 in *The Rotarian*, the official magazine of Rotary International.

In 1936, at the Olympics in Berlin, Germany, I saw the basketball teams of 21 nations line up, each behind the flag of its own country, and I had the privilege of speaking a few words of greeting, and of congratulating them on the part they were about to have in promoting international goodwill.

As I talked to those superb athletes from all quarters of the globe, I realized that the game I had invented back at the Springfield, Massachusetts, Y.M.C.A. College almost 45 years before had had a fine part in the development of better international understanding. I was more convinced of the good effects of the game when the accident of the draw paired China and Japan for a first-day game—with the memories of the Manchukuo still vivid. And a Chinese refereed the final game of the series, between the United States and Canada. If added evidence were needed, it could have been found in the dinner attended by 19 alumni of the Springfield College, men of many nationalities and all from the coaching staffs of the basketball teams at the Olympic games.

It was indeed fortunate for the game that it was devised at the Y.M.C.A. College, for this insured its early and widespread adoption. The prospective leaders of the youth, in school at Springfield, found the game interesting, and they took it with them as they spread to their tasks as Y.M.C.A. secretaries throughout the United States, or became missionaries in other lands. Bob Gailey, who had been a center on the Princeton University football team, took the new game with him to Tientsin, China, in 1894, and Charles Siler, a University of Kansas graduate of 1916, revived the game there. Duncan Patton took the game to India, also in 1894; Emil Thies to France in 1895; Ishakawa to Japan in 1900. C. Harek, another "Y" man, introduced the game into Persia (now Iran) in 1901. American soldiers played it in China during the Boxer rebellion, and in The Philippines when the 20th Kansas Regiment was there under Fred Funston. For many years a Far East tournament brought together the best basketball players of China, Japan, and The Philippines.

Invention of the game of basketball was not an accident. It was developed to meet a need.

After my first year at the Y.M.C.A. College, I was put on the staff, for I had had gymnasium experience at McGill University, Montreal, Quebec, Canada. One of my duties at Springfield was with a class of 18 prospective "Y" secretaries. No problems arose so long as we could get out of doors for exercise, but when Winter came, my worries began. Those boys simply would not play drop the handkerchief!

Dr. Luther Gulick, head of the school, put the problem squarely up to me, and kept bringing the matter up in faculty meeting, until I realized I really had to do something about it. Dr. Gulick had reminded me on one occasion that there is nothing new under the sun—what appears new is just a new combination of older things. So I began to recall my boyhood games, and to study the problem in that light.

In our outdoor games we had been running with a football. Stopping the runner involved tackling, and that would be too dangerous on a gymnasium floor. I decided the ball must be thrown.

But a small ball thrown or passed might be hurled with dangerous force, so I used a larger ball, choosing at first a soccer ball, since one was at hand. Very early, manufacturers provided specially designed balls for our game.

I recalled also from my boyhood in Canada that when we played the game called duck on a rock, a hurled ball might send the "duck" farther, but the tossed ball was far more accurate. My new game, I decided, must have the ball tossed at the goal. Now, a goal on the floor would be too easy to guard, so I decided on a box above the floor. The janitor couldn't find a box, but he offered a couple of peach baskets, which were nailed to the gymnasium railing. That rail was ten feet from the floor, and so strong is tradition that it is almost heresy to suggest change, even in these days of players of 6 feet 6 inches and more.

The Canadian game of lacrosse suggested the positions, and so for several years the newspaper accounts carried the lineups with players in these positions: home, right forward, left forward, center, right center, left center, goal, right back, left back.

"Just another game!" was the first exclamation when the 18 secretaries-to-be came for their exercise. I divided the squad and started the game. It took.

The school paper described the game in January, 1892, and the New York *Times* in April, 1892, had a story about the "new game" that was being played in gymnasiums that Spring. "Y" secretaries in other cities wrote for more information about the game. In that way C. O. Bemis learned of it, and started it at Geneva College, Beaver Falls, Pennsylvania. In the same way, H. F. Kanlenberg, who had left Springfield in 1890, introduced it at the University of Iowa early in 1892. I interested the young men in the game when I was at medical school in Denver, Colorado, between 1894 and 1898, and, of course, I introduced the game at Kansas when I came to that institution in the Fall of 1898. Thus the game spread.

One of my classmates at Springfield in 1890 was Alonzo Stagg, later to become the famous football coach at the University of Chicago, and now at the College of the Pacific. About the time I was finishing my medical course at Gross School, now the medical school of the University of Colorado, Stagg met Francis Huntington Snow, of the University of Kansas. Chancellor Snow was looking for a combination man—one who could direct the physical-education work and at the same time conduct the daily chapel exercises. Stagg recalled that I had prepared for the ministry at McGill University and had turned to the Y.M.C.A. only because I thought the opportunities for helping young men lay more through exercise than through preaching; and so he recommended me. I have been at the University of Kansas ever since.

Strangely enough, though I qualified and was ordained as a Presbyterian minister, and have an M.D. degree, I have never held a pastorate, nor have I put out a physician's shingle. The nearest to preaching came in Y.M.C.A. service with the 20th Kansas on the Mexican border and in two years of service with the "Y" in France. And the preaching was rather indirect, at that. For example, we found that too many of the boys from our camp were going into a near-by town and getting into all kinds of devilment. We set up a boxing ring near the camp entrance, and would start a lively match about the time the boys began starting on "leave." They stopped to watch; then begged for a chance to participate; and the next thing they knew it was time to be back in quarters. Prize fights may sound like strange preaching, but they did work.

Exercise came naturally to me, for I had grown up in the lumber camps near my native Almonte, Ontario, Canada. The two and a half miles to high school through snow and subzero weather offered no child's play. As I recall, I was much like the other boys, getting into fisticuffs occasionally and taking part in all the games. It took eight battles to get the better of one lad. When it seemed I was going with a rough crowd in high school, I quit, but I had lots of time to think as I drove the lead team on my uncle's woodlot. My parent had died when I was 8 and I decided I must go to college. I even aspired to become a preacher. Therefore, I completed my high-school work and entered McGill. In return for Summer work on the farm, my uncle made possible my attendance at McGill, and I dug into my studies with vim.

One evening a couple of upperclassmen came to my room to admonish me to take more exercise, and to urge that I attend the gymnasium classes. I laughed them off until they had gone, but decided there might be something to their advice. I went to gym class the next night, seized a pair of Indian clubs, and took a place in front of the instructor. Later I learned that he reserved the front rank for his more proficient pupils. Death of a gym instructor a short time later opened a place for me on the staff, and provided for the ministerial year in the seminary.

It was while playing football at McGill that I received one of my strongest urges to make athletics become an avenue of preaching.

One day in practice something went wrong, and the guard next to me let loose a stream of profanity. Suddenly he stopped and exclaimed: "Excuse me, Jim. I'm sorry."

I hadn't said a thing; in fact, I had hardly noticed his swearing, for I had heard some pretty fancy profanity in the Canadian lumber camps. However, the incident set me thinking, and I talked to the Y.M.C.A. secretary about it. He told me of the Springfield College, and I was all for moving to Springfield right then. Another faculty member persuaded me to complete my course.

For about 47 years now I have watched my game expand in appeal to the young men and women of the world. The 13 simple rules have been expanded into a whole book, going into minute detail, but with one exception these large books retain all the principles of the original rules. I don't know how many languages are now used for the rules books, but I have, supplementing my file of American and Canadian rules, books printed for use in Germany, France, Uruguay, Paraguay, Arabia, Spain, Portugal, Madagascar, China, and Japan.

I have watched the shifting of the rules from year to year as need was found for more explicit directions. In late years I have noted the adoption of the ten-second rule, requiring play to move promptly into the forward court, and, more recently, the abolition of the center jump, except at the start of each half. Some of the changes have been improvements; some I question.

One of the reasons I am sorry to see the center jump relegated to a subordinate place is that it takes from the game one of the large elements of suspense—something desirable in any sport. Which, do you think, appeals to the spectator the more: the actual dropping of the ball through the basket, or the suspense—the seconds when one wonders if the ball is going in? Fred Pralle, who won national recognition at the University of Kansas last season, had an uncanny way of throwing from far down the sidelines, a perfect shot, but one taking many fractions of a second in the making. Even more breath taking was another Kansan, Paul Rogers, of a few years ago. He likewise shot from far down the sidelines. It would look like a good shot, then appear to be going wide. Just as the spectators had decided the ball would miss, it would strike the backboard and rebound squarely for a score.

In the same way, there is suspense in the center jump, and some pretty plays have been built about the uncertainty there. Though the taller center seemed to have the advantage, it was not always true; often the shorter man was the better on the jump. Moreover, one of my technical studies of the game showed that in at least half the cases the team that failed to get the jump would recover the ball within three or four plays and score. Mere possession of the ball through the tipoff earns few points—the ball has to be tossed into the basket. For that reason I have always maintained that the team with the ball is not to be blamed for stalling. It is the business of the players on the defense to go in there and get the ball. If they don't, it is they who are stalling.

Basketball coaches have become more and more proficient, some developing the "man to man" defense and others the "zone" system. The more I watch the game, the more I realize that, while easy to understand and simple to demonstrate, it is nevertheless a challenge to skill. It is only through thorough grounding in the fundamentals and constant practice that championships are won. This challenge to perfection in execution of the play is, to my mind, one of the attractions of the game for the pure pleasure it brings to the players.

Just how many persons engage in the game of basketball, no one knows, but the number must be large. I am told that 90 percent of the high schools in America have basketball teams. Churches, clubs, neighborhood gangs, have their squads of five—a number adopted within a few years. The original nine was half the class, but was too many for most gym floors. The tiniest hamlets now have their teams, and in many rural school yards is even a simple basket on a pole, with the boys playing on the bare earth. I have no doubts about the estimate of 18 million players every Winter.

Basketball is so generally played in gymnasiums in the United States that one hardly realizes that it is played out of doors in Germany and Japan and other countries. In Japan wooden platforms are often erected, but in Germany the outdoor courts are paved with a combination of salt, sand, and sawdust which, when wet, is not unlike the sea beach when the tide is out. That final Olympic basketball game I mentioned earlier was played on such a court in a pouring rain, despite the fact that a great gymnasium stood empty near at hand.

Basketball, finally, is a popular spectators' game. How many millions the world over gather to cheer their favorite teams is beyond a guess. But this much is certain: In the United States for several years basketball has attracted more customers than either football or baseball, amateur and professional combined. Collectors of statistics say that some 90 million admissions were paid to see the youth of the nation perform on basketball courts last year. And with constantly increasing seating capacity being made available, the years ahead will probably witness even a higher total. When one notes in the public prints that crowds of 18,000 fans gather in Madison Square Garden in New York City for important contests, he will admit the game of basketball has made quite an advance in interest since the day when a small group of young men first tossed a ball into a couple of peach baskets nailed to a gymnasium railing.

We *the People* Radio Program Interview

January 31, 1939

A radio interview transcript of James Naismith as part of the We *the People* radio program hosted in New York by Gabriel Heatter. This is believed to be the only existing audio recording of Naismith, who was in New York to watch basketball at Madison Square Garden.

HEATTER: Tomorrow night fifteen thousand cheering fans will pack Madison Square Garden in New York City to witness a giant basketball doubleheader. In that cheering crowd, sitting in row C, seat 11 will be a modest seventy-seven-year-old man. Those fans won't know that he made possible the game they are watching. But you're going to meet him now. Sanka Coffee has brought him here tonight all the way from Lawrence, Kansas. Dr. James A. Naismith, the inventor of basketball. Dr. Naismith, how did you happen to invent basketball?

NAISMITH: Well, Mr. Heatter, it was in the winter of 1891 when I was physical instructor at Springfield College in Massachusetts. We had a real New England blizzard. For days, the students couldn't go outdoors, so they began roughhousing in the halls. We tried everything to keep them quiet. We tried playing a modified form of football in the gymnasium, but they got bored with that. Something had to be done. One day I had an idea. I called the boys to the gym, divided them up into teams of nine and gave them an old soccer ball. I showed them two peach baskets I had nailed up at each end of the gym, and I told them the idea was to throw the ball into the opposing team's peach basket. I blew a whistle, and the first game of basketball began.

HEATTER: And what rules did you have for your new game, Dr. Naismith?

NAISMITH: Well, I didn't have enough, and that's where I made my big mistake. The boys began attacking, kicking and punching in the clinches. They ended up in a free-for-all in the middle of the gym floor. Before I could pull them apart, one boy was knocked out, several of them had black eyes, and one had a dislocated shoulder. It certainly was murder. Well after that first match, I was afraid they would kill each other. But they kept nagging me to let them play again, so I made up some more rules. The most important one was that there should be no running with the ball. That stopped tackling and slugging. We tried out the game with those rules, and we didn't have one casualty. We had a fine, clean sport. Ten years later, basketball was being played all over the country. And in 1936, I saw it played for the first time at the Olympic Games. And the whole thing started with a couple of peach baskets I put up in a little gym forty-eight years ago. I guess it just goes to show what you can do if you have to.

Letter to Bruce Etchison

February 24, 1939

Letter written by James Naismith to Bruce Etchison on February 24, 1939, in which he discusses the early size of the courts, the original rules, and the equipment.

University of Kansas
Lawrence

2./24./ '39.

Mr. Bruce Etchison
Washington D.C.

My dear Sir:-

Basketball was first played with nine men on a side, and in a gymnasium 45 x 65 feet with a gallery running around it.

The game was very simple at that time. There were 13 rules 12 of which are now in the rules and I often wish that the 13th were still in. It prohibited the player from handling the ball with any part of the body with the hands only. This would eliminate diving for the ball when it is free on the floor.

The only equipment we had in the first few games were a Soccer ball and a couple of peach baskets. We wore the regulation gymnasium uniform Long trousers and quarter sleeve jerseys, with elk sole shoes.

I have frequently been asked to put on a game resembling the first one. I have asked that they find 18 young men 23 to 30 years of age, with moustaches and who had never seen read or heard of a game of basketball and then I could put on a good representation of the first game. Whenever I have tried to do this the players have injected the new rules or have gone to the other extreme and have made it rougher than football.

This is not to discourage you from putting such a game on but to show you that it is necessary to have a good many rehearsals to get anything like a true representation. Get your men 9 on a side line them up three forwards three centers and three guards and tell them to pass the ball never to dribble it. Have the guards keep their places in the back court and to feed the ball forward as rapidly as possible.

If fouls are made for the first warn the player and for the second personal foul put him on the side lines until the next goal is made. No substitute allowed. The goal will count one and no foul throws.

I will be in New York Mar 15th at the Madison Square Gardens at the final Tournament. If any of your men happen to be there at that time I will be glad to answer any questions you may care to ask.

Most sincerely yours
James Naismith
1515 University Drive.

Memorandum of Conference

March 23, 1939

This is a memorandum of a conference between James Naismith and Dean W. Peterson on March 23, 1939, at the Hotel Lincoln in New York City.

Springfield College
Corporate Name
International Young Men's Christian Association
Springfield, Massachusetts

March 29, 1939

Memorandum recorded by Mr. Dean W. Peterson of conference with Dr. James Naismith at Hotel Lincoln in New York City on March 23, 1939.

Dr. Naismith unfolded in unreserved intimacy his deepest motives and aspirations for his remaining years and is anxious to cooperate with Springfield College to make his time count for the betterment of humanity. "Now I want for the remaining years to give the best I have to humanity." "Living my life now in such a way as to give the benefit of my rich experiences for the uplift of others." "Recognition of the accumulative good of basketball, and do not desire personal tribute." "I don't want anything for myself."

He spoke of having the original manuscript giving the first rules and that application has been made for these by the British Museum, by the Smithsonian Institute Library, and by Kansas University. Dr. Naismith's statement was that "I want this document to be placed permanently where it can do the most good and have, therefore, decided to give it to Springfield College." "As long as Springfield College stands in its unique place and influence, that is where I want to help. I believe physical education in the sense in which it is interpreted at Springfield College is basic, and the game is for the students, not for the spectators."

He then discussed Basketball Recognition. The personalities he suggested to give backing and aid for our recognition program to culminate the fiftieth anniversary of basketball in 1941 were Lomax, "There's a boy you can pin to"; Griffith, "a particular friend of mine at Drake, the Czar of Big Ten and he has been president also of the NBA."; Mr. Irish of Madison Square Garden "a key boy for basketball"; Lonberg. The three major groups: "the Eastern Intercollegiate, the Big Ten, and the Big Six." He cited the three main bodies governing basketball as:

1) A. A. U. National Basketball Committee, which puts on the tournament at Denver.

2) The National Inter-collegiate Basketball group.

3) The National Collegiate Basketball group

Mr. Ferris, Woolworth Building, New York, is head of the first

Mr. Emil Liston of Baker University is head of the second

Coach Olson of Ohio State is head of the third.

The sports writers of New York have been friendly to Dr. Naismith and to the idea of recognizing Dr. Naismith as the originator of the game and the Fiftieth Anniversary of the game in 1941. This interest has been evidenced primarily on the part of Everett Morris and Stan Lomax.

Dr. Naismith thinks highly of Grantland Rice who is, without a doubt, the dean of present day sports writers. He said that Rice entered the sports field as a basketball player. It would, of course, be very worthwhile for the right person to talk with Grantland Rice about it.

Program of cultivation of the field to proceed continuously from now on until culmination. Dr. Naismith wants to give his time without remuneration except the extra travel costs, is ready to be scheduled anywhere, is planning trips for this spring and summer, and will give his time on any schedule that may be developed to lay foundations for the fiftieth anniversary of basketball.

He feels that there are hundreds of places that have little appreciation of the character building values of basketball. He suggests that talks and informal groups and special dinners will spread the story like the spokes of a wheel. Advises immediate action and does not believe that this can be postponed if it is to culminate successfully in an adequate fund for the field house.

He thinks we must have a man giving his whole time for direct personal contact in addition to the ground work which Dr. Naismith is willing to follow through on the schedules which we lay out for him. He is ready to follow the routing that we may lay out for the Northwest in June of this year, speaking at YMCA's, colleges, high-school groups, etc. He is willing to have us use as a news story, if we think it is of value, his securing a degree of D.D. at the Seminary associated with McGill.

He referred to Jones as a good alumnus for us in Europe, Summers in South America, and Buck in India.

He stated that the Japanese had informed him that Japan calls basketball its national game.

The Origin of Basketball

———

1941

James Naismith's book *Basketball: Its Origin and Development* was published in 1941, two years after his death. Chapter 3 is entitled "The Origin of Basketball."

Two weeks had almost passed since I had taken over the troublesome class. The time was almost gone; in a day or two I would have to report to the faculty the success or failure of my attempts. So far they had all been failures, and it seemed to me that I had exhausted my resources. The prospect before me was, to say the least, discouraging. How I hated the thought of going back to the group and admitting that, after all my theories, I, too, had failed to hold the interest of the class. It was worse than losing a game. All the stubbornness of my Scotch ancestry was aroused, all my pride of achievement urged me on; I would not go back and admit that I had failed.

The day before my two weeks ended I met the class. I will always remember that meeting. I had nothing new to try and no idea of what I was going to do. The class period passed with little order, and at the end of the hour the boys left the gym. I can still see that group of fellows filing out the door. As that last pair of grey pants vanished into the locker room, I saw the end of all my ambitions and hopes.

With weary footsteps I mounted the flight of narrow stairs that led to my office directly over the locker room. I slumped down in my chair, my head in my hands and my elbows on the desk. I was a thoroughly disheartened and discouraged young instructor. Below me, I could hear the boys in the locker room having a good time; they were giving expression to the very spirit that I had tried so hard to evoke.

I had been a student the year before, and I could picture the group in that locker room. A towel would snap and some fellow would jerk erect and try to locate the guilty individual. Some of it was rough play, but it was all in fun, and each of them entered into it with that spirit. There would be talking and jesting, and I could even imagine the things that the group would be saying about my efforts. I was sure that the fellows did not dislike me, but I was just as sure that they felt that I had given them nothing better than the other instructors.

As I listened to the noise in the room below, my discouragement left me. I looked back over my attempts to see, if possible, the cause of my failures. I passed in review the gymnastic games that I had tried, and I saw that they were impossible. They were really children's games; the object that was to be obtained changed with each play, and no man could be interested in this type of game. It was necessary to have some permanent objective that would keep the minds of the participants active and interested.

As I thought of the other games that I had tried, I realized that the normal individual is strongly influenced by tradition. If he is interested in a game, any attempt to modify that game sets up an antagonism in his mind. I realized that any attempt to change the known games would necessarily result in failure. It was evident that a new principle was necessary; but how to evolve this principle was beyond my ken.

As I sat there at my desk, I began to study games from the philosophical side. I had been taking one game at a time and had failed to find what I was looking for. This time I would take games as a whole and study them.

My first generalization was that all team games used a ball of some kind; therefore, any new game must have a ball. Two kinds of balls were used at that time, one large and the other small. I noted that all games that used a small ball had some intermediate equipment with which to handle it. Cricket and baseball had bats, lacrosse and hockey had sticks, tennis and squash had rackets. In each of these games, the use of the intermediate equipment made the game more difficult to learn. The Americans were at sea with a lacrosse stick, and the Canadians could not use a baseball bat.

The game that we sought would be played by many; therefore, it must be easy to learn. Another objection to a small ball was that it could be easily hidden. It would be difficult for a group to play a game in which the ball was in sight only part of the time.

I then considered a large ball that could be easily handled and which almost anyone could catch and throw with very little practice. I decided that the ball should be large and light, one that could be easily handled and yet could not be concealed. There were two balls of this kind then in use, one the spheroid of Rugby and the other the round ball of soccer. It was not until later that I decided which one of these two I would select.

The type of ball being settled, I turned next to the point of interest of various games. I concluded that the most interesting game at that time was American Rugby. I asked myself why this game could not be used as an indoor sport. The answer to this was easy. It was because tackling was necessary in Rugby. But why was tackling necessary? Again the answer was easy. It was because the men were allowed to run with the ball, and it was necessary to stop them. With these facts in mind, I sat erect at my desk and said aloud:

"If he can't run with the ball, we don't have to tackle; and if we don't have to tackle, the roughness will be eliminated."

I can still recall how I snapped my fingers and shouted,

"I've got it!"

This time I felt that I really had a new principle for a game, one that would not violate any tradition. On looking back, it was hard to see why I was so elated. I had as yet nothing but a single idea, but I was sure that the rest would work out correctly.

Starting with the idea that the player in possession of the ball could not run with it, the next step was to see just what he could do with it. There was little choice in this respect. It would be necessary for him to throw it or bat it with his hand. In my mind, I began to play a game and to visualize the movements of the players. Suppose that a player was running, and a teammate threw the ball to him. Realizing that it would be impossible for him to stop immediately, I made this exception: when a man was running and received the ball, he must make an honest effort to stop or else pass the ball immediately. This was the second step of the game.

In my mind I was still sticking to the traditions of the older games, especially football. In that game, the ball could be thrown in any direction except forward. In this new game, however, the player with the ball could not advance, and I saw no reason why he should not be allowed to throw or bat it in any direction. So far, I had a game that was played with a large light ball; the players could not run with the ball, but must pass it or bat it with the hands; and the pass could be made in any direction.

As I mentally played the game, I remembered that I had seen two players in a soccer game, both after the ball. One player attempted to head the ball just as the other player kicked at it. The result was a badly gashed head for the first man. I then turned this incident to the new game. I could imagine one player attempting to strike the ball with his fist and, intentionally or otherwise, coming in contact with another player's face. I then decided that the fist must not be used in striking the ball.

The game now had progressed only to the point where it was "keep away," and my experience with gymnastic games convinced me that it would not hold the interest of the players.

The next step was to devise some objective for the players. In all existing games there was some kind of a goal, and I felt that this was essential. I thought of the different games, in the hope that I might be able to use one of their goals. Football had a goal line, over which the ball must be carried, and goal posts, over which the ball might be kicked. Soccer, lacrosse, and hockey had goals into which the ball might be driven. Tennis and badminton had marks on the court inside which the ball must be kept. Thinking of all these, I mentally placed a goal like the one used in lacrosse at each end of the floor.

A lacrosse goal is simply a space six feet high and eight feet wide. The players attempt to throw the ball into this space; the harder the ball is thrown, the more chance to make a goal. I was sure that this play would lead to roughness, and I did not want that. I thought of limiting the sweep of the arms or of having the ball delivered from in front of the person, but I knew that many would resent my limiting the power of the player.

By what line of association it occurred to me I do not know, but I was back in Bennie's Corners, Ontario, playing Duck on the Rock. I could remember distinctly the large rock back of the blacksmith shop, about as high as our knees and as large around as a wash tub. Each of us would get a "duck," a stone about as large as our two doubled fists. About twenty feet from the large rock we would draw a base line, and then in various manners we would choose one of the group to be guard, or "it."

To start the game, the guard placed his duck on the rock, and we behind the base line attempted to knock it off by throwing our ducks. More often than not, when we threw our ducks we missed, and if we went to retrieve them, the guard tagged us; then one of us had to change places with him. If, however, someone knocked the guard's "duck" off the rock, he had to replace it before he could tag anyone.

It came distinctly to my mind that some of the boys threw their ducks as hard as they could; when they missed, the ducks were far from the base. When they went to retrieve them, they had farther to run and had more chance of being tagged. On the other hand, if the duck was tossed in an arc, it did not go so far. If the guard's duck was hit, it fell on the far side of the rock, whereas the one that was thrown bounced nearer the base and was easily caught up before the guard replaced his. When the duck was thrown in an arc, accuracy was more effective than force.

With this game in mind, I thought that if the goal were horizontal instead of vertical, the players would be compelled to throw the ball in an arc; and force, which made for roughness, would be of no value.

A horizontal goal, then, was what I was looking for, and I pictured it in my mind. I would place a box at either end of the floor, and each time the ball entered the box it would count as a goal. There was one thing, however, that I had overlooked. If nine men formed a defense around the goal, it would be impossible for the ball to enter it; but if I placed the goal above the players' heads, this type of defense would be useless. The only chance that the guards would have would be to go out and get the ball before the opponents had an opportunity to throw for goal.

I had a team game with equipment and an objective. My problem now was how to start it. Again I reviewed the games with which I was familiar. I found that the intent of starting any game was to give each side an equal chance to obtain the ball. I thought of water polo, where the teams were lined up at the ends of the pool and at a signal the ball was thrown into the center. There was always a mad scramble to gain possession of the ball, and it took only an instant for me to reject this plan. I could see nine men at each end of the gym, all making a rush for the ball as it was thrown into the center of the floor; and I winced as I thought of the results of that collision.

I then turned to the game of English Rugby. When the ball went out of bounds on the side line, it was taken by the umpire and thrown in between two lines of forward players. This was somewhat like polo, but the players had no chance to run at each other. As I thought of this method of starting the game, I remembered one incident that happened to me. In a game with Queen's College, the ball was thrown between the two lines of players. I took one step and went high in the air. I got the ball all right, but as I came down I landed on a shoulder that was shoved into my midriff. I decided that this method would not do. I did feel, though, that if the roughness could be eliminated, that tossing up the ball between two teams was the fairest way of starting a game. I reasoned that if I picked only one player from each team and threw the ball up between them, there would be little chance for roughness. I realize now how seriously I underestimated the ingenuity of the American boy.

When I had decided how I would start the game, I felt that I would have little trouble. I knew that there would be questions to be met; but I had the fundamental principles of a game, and I was more than willing to try to meet these problems. I continued with my day's work, and it was late in the evening before I again had a chance to think of my new scheme. I believe that I am the first person who ever played basketball; and although I used the bed for a court, I certainly played a hard game that night.

The following morning I went into my office, thinking of the new game. I had not yet decided what ball I should use. Side by side on the floor lay two balls, one a football and the other a soccer ball.

I noticed the lines of the football and realized that it was shaped so that it might be carried in the arms. There was to be no carrying of the ball in this new game, so I walked over, picked up the soccer ball, and started in search of a goal.

As I walked down the hall, I met Mr. Stebbins, the superintendent of the buildings. I asked him if he had two boxes about eighteen inches square. Stebbins thought a minute, and then said:

"No, I haven't any boxes, but I'll tell you what I do have. I have two old peach baskets down in the store room, if they will do you any good."

I told him to bring them up, and a few minutes later he appeared with the two baskets tucked under his arm. They were round and somewhat larger at the top than at the bottom. I found a hammer and some nails and tacked the baskets to the lower rail of the balcony, one at either end of the gym.

I was almost ready to try the new game, but I felt that I needed a set of rules, in order that the men would have some guide. I went to my office, pulled out a scratch pad, and set to work. The rules were so clear in my mind that in less than an hour I took my copy to Miss Lyons, our stenographer, who typed the following set of thirteen rules.

The ball to be an ordinary *Association* football.

1. The ball may be thrown in any direction with one or both hands.
2. The ball may be batted in any direction with one or both hands (never with the fist).
3. A player cannot run with the ball. The player must throw it from the spot on which he catches it; allowance to be made for a man who catches the ball when running at a good speed.
4. The ball must be held in or between the hands; the arms or body must not be used for holding it.
5. No shouldering, holding, pushing, tripping, or striking, in any way the person of an opponent shall be allowed; the first

infringement of this rule by any person shall count as a foul, the second shall disqualify him until the next goal is made, or, if there was an evident intent to injure the person for the whole of the game, no substitute allowed.

6. A foul is striking at the ball with the fist, violation of Rules 3, 4, and such as described in Rule 5.

7. If either side makes three consecutive fouls, it shall count a goal for the opponents. (Consecutive means without the opponents in the meantime making a foul.)

8. A goal shall be made when the ball is thrown or batted from the grounds into the basket and stays there, providing those defending the goal do not touch or disturb the goal. If the ball rests on the edge and the opponent moves the basket, it shall count as a goal.

9. When the ball goes out of bounds, it shall be thrown into the field and played by the person first touching it. In case of a dispute, the umpire shall throw it straight into the field. The thrower-in is allowed five seconds. If he holds it longer it shall go to the opponent. If any side persists in delaying the game, the umpire shall call a foul on them.

10. The umpire shall be judge of the men and shall note the fouls and notify the referee when three consecutive fouls have been made. He shall have power to disqualify men according to Rule 5.

11. The referee shall be judge of the ball and shall decide when the ball is in play, in bounds, to which side it belongs, and shall keep the time. He shall decide when a goal has been made, and keep account of the goals, with any other duties that are usually performed by a referee.

12. The time shall be two fifteen minute halves, with five minutes rest between.

13. The side making the most goals in that time shall be declared the winners. In case of a draw, the game may, by agreement of the captains be continued until another goal is made.

When Miss Lyons finished typing the rules, it was almost class time, and I was anxious to get down to the gym. I took the rules and made my way down the stairs. Just inside the door there was a bulletin board for notices. With thumb tacks I fastened the rules to this board and then walked across the gym. I was sure in my own mind that the game was good, but it needed a real test. I felt that its success or failure depended largely on the way that the class received it.

The first member of the class to arrive was Frank Mahan. He was a southerner from North Carolina, had played tackle on the football team, and was the ringleader of the group. He saw me standing with a ball in my hand and perhaps surmised that another experiment was to be tried. He looked up at the basket on one end of the gallery, and then his eyes turned to me. He gazed at me for an instant, and then looked toward the other end of the gym. Perhaps I was nervous, because his exclamation sounded like a death knell as he said,

"Huh! another new game!"

When the class arrived, I called the roll and told them that I had another game, which I felt sure would be good. I promised them that if this was a failure, I would not try any more experiments. I then read the rules from the bulletin board and proceeded to organize the game.

There were eighteen men in the class; I selected two captains and had them choose sides. When the teams were chosen, I placed the men on the floor. There were three forwards, three centers, and three backs on each team. I chose two of the center men to jump, then threw the ball between them. It was the start of the first basketball game and the finish of the trouble with that class.

As was to be expected, they made a great many fouls at first; and as a foul was penalized by putting the offender on the side lines until the next goal was made, sometimes half of a team would be in the penalty area. It was simply a case of no one knowing just what to do. There was no team work, but each man did his best. The forwards tried to make goals and the backs tried to keep the opponents from making them. The team was large, and the floor was small. Any man on the field was close enough to the basket to throw for goal, and most of them were anxious to score. We tried, however, to develop team work by having the guards pass the ball to the forwards.

The game was a success from the time that the first ball was tossed up. The players were interested and seemed to enjoy the game. Word soon got around that they were having fun in Naismith's gym class, and only a few days after the first game we began to have a gallery.

The class met at eleven-thirty in the morning, and the game was in full swing by twelve o'clock. Some teachers from Buckingham Grade School were passing the gym one day, and hearing the noise, decided to investigate. They could enter the gallery through a door that led to the street. Each day after that, they stopped to watch the game, sometimes becoming so interested that they would not have time to get their lunch. These teachers came to me one day and asked me why girls could not play that game. I told them that I saw no reason why they should not, and this group organized the first girls' basketball team.

It is little wonder that the crowd enjoyed the game. If we could see it today as it was played then, we would laugh too. The players were all mature men; most of them had mustaches, and one or two had full beards. Their pants were long, and their shirts had short sleeves. Sometimes when a player received the ball, he would poise with it over his head to make sure that he would make the goal. About the time that he was ready to throw, someone would reach up from behind and take the ball out of his hands. This occurred frequently and was a never-ending source of amusement. No matter how often a player lost the ball in this manner, he would always look around with a surprised expression that would plainly say, "Who did that?" His embarrassment only added to the laughter of the crowd.

It was shortly after the first game that Frank Mahan came to me before class hour and said:

"You remember the rules that were put on the bulletin board?"

"Yes, I do," I answered.

"They disappeared," he said.

"I know it," I replied.

"Well, I took them," Frank said. "I knew that this game would be a success, and I took them as a souvenir, but I think now that you should have them."

Mahan told me that the rules were in his trunk and that he would bring them down later. That afternoon he entered my office and handed me the two typewritten sheets. I still have them, and they are one of my prized possessions.

At the Christmas vacation a number of the students went home and some of them started the game in their local Y.M.C.A.'s. There were no printed rules at that time, and each student played the game as he remembered it. It was not until January, 1892, that the school paper, called the *Triangle*, first printed the rules under the heading, "A New Game."

One day after the students returned from their vacation, the same Frank Mahan came to me and asked me what I was going to call the game. I told him that I had not thought of the matter but was interested only in getting it started. Frank insisted that it must have a name and suggested the name of Naismith ball. I laughed and told him that I thought the name would kill any game. Frank then said:

"Why not call it basketball?"

"We have a basket and a ball, and it seems to me that would be a good name for it," I replied. It was in this way that basketball was named.

When the first game had ended, I felt that I could now go to Doctor Gulick and tell him that I had accomplished the two seemingly impossible tasks that he had assigned to me: namely, to interest the class in physical exercise and to invent a new game.

Duck on a Rock Rules

—————

No Date

1. Find yourself a good stone
2. Make one person "the guard" who will put his stone on top of the large rock
3. Everyone else must line up about 15 feet away from the large rock
4. Each person in line takes turns throwing their stone at the "guard's" stone trying to knock it off the rock
5. If you knock the "guard's" stone off, then the "guard" would go to the end of the line and wait for his turn to throw
6. If you miss, you have to run and get your stone before the "guard" can tag you
7. If you get tagged, then you become the "guard"

2

Physical Education

The assignment that led to Naismith's invention of the game of basketball was part of a physical education course that Dr. Luther Gulick was offering. New notions of physical education, health, and religion were gaining greater currency in the 1870s and 1880s. The notion of physical education is integrated in much of Naismith's writings and speeches about the game, and he ultimately believed that the game of basketball reflected the new movement of Muscular Christianity. His belief in basketball as a form of activity to strengthen the mind, body, and spirit never waivered throughout his life even as the game became a commercial success, a fact of the game's inevitable evolution that he did not foresee. Nearly two decades after he invented the game, Naismith wrote a pamphlet, *Fundamentals of Basketball*, published by the Rawlings Manufacturing Company. In addition to describing the game, Naismith wrote about how basketball could serve, in a positive fashion, different communities such as rural schools, grade schools, churches, industrial organizations, and girls. These attributes and the physical benefits of playing the game were fundamental to his thinking and did not change much during his lifetime. This is evident in his interview with Dr. Phog Allen, dean of coaching and head basketball coach at the University of Kansas. This interview was conducted in 1938, a year before Naismith died. His belief in basketball and its role in physical education is also reflected in the Naismith circular to public educators.

Fundamentals of Basketball

1910

> *Fundamentals of Basketball* was a pamphlet published by the Rawlings Manufacturing Company in 1910. The pamphlet was written by James Naismith.

JAMES NAISMITH, UNIVERSITY of KANSAS, The INVENTOR and FATHER of BASKETBALL, *Says*:

> I have tested the Rawlings-Naismith Basketballs by all the means at my command, such as the calipers, the scales, the tapeline, by rolling, bouncing and in general practice and find that it meets all the requirements of a superior Basketball.
>
> I believe that it is a decided advance in Basketball construction.

ATTRIBUTES DEVELOPED BY BASKETBALL

Basketball is not now, nor was it ever intended to be, a complete system of physical education. Its main purpose was recreation and development of certain factors that are particularly developed by games. It was intended primarily for young men who had acquired their physical development. Its place in a system of physical education is to develop certain factors that are not obtained by manual labor, or heavy work of any kind.

On account of the fact that it is intrinsically interesting it has, in many cases, been substituted for all other forms of motor activity. This is an error, especially with young boys, in a system of physical education.

Basketball has a place in a scheme of physical education, first, because it is attractive in itself, and second, because it develops certain attributes as well, if not better, than most other forms of physical activity. These attributes are mainly development of the nerve control of the individual rather than the development of brawn. Games have been called the laboratory for the development of ethical and moral attributes, and they may become such if properly conducted.

The attributes that can be best developed by Basketball are:

1. Agility, or the power of the body to put itself into any position with quickness, ease and accuracy. This is especially developed by the movements of the body to elude the opponent, keep the ball away from him, get into a position to make a pass, a shot, or a dribble.

2. Accuracy—Goals are made by passing a ten inch ball through an eighteen inch opening set at a right angle to the backboard, and ten feet in the air. In order to do this it is necessary to give the ball the right direction, the right elevation, to let go of the ball at the right time—all of which makes for extreme accuracy.

3. Alertness—In some games there may be a letting down of attention as no further activity occurs until a signal is given, but in basketball the attention must be in such a condition as to be ready to operate at any time. The ball travels about so fast that the player must be awake and ready to act at any time while the game is in progress.

4. Cooperation—In no other game is cooperation so necessary as there are only five players and each is dependent on the other players. Two players cooperating can always beat one, three can beat two, four can beat three, and if one does not cooperate, the team is one man short.

5. Initiative—In basketball it is impossible to plan what the next move is going to be, consequently the player must react to the conditions without time to make up his mind as to which is the best plan. When he meets an entirely new condition he cannot depend on the coach to tell him, but must meet the emergency until he has time to formulate a plan of procedure.

I consider this one of the most valuable attributes, and the present dependence on the coach destroys this attribute.

6. Skill—In few games that are easy to learn is there need for so great an amount of skill. Skill is the ability to use the right muscle groups at the time when they are most needed, and in the proper sequence, and with the correct amount of force, and this with a moving team mate and against a moving opponent.

7. Reflex judgment—This is the ability to make the arms and legs do the right thing without a mental process to tell which of several things to do. The eye sees an open space towards which a team mate is running and the ball is passed in such a way that he is able to get it in the most favorable position to pass, shoot, or dribble. The Kansas University record for sight and touch reaction is held by basketball men. No prettier sight can be seen in athletics than one player touching the ball to another, who touches it to a third, who tosses it into the goal, the whole done quicker than the mind could possibly devise the play.

8. Speed—The ability to move the body from one location to another in the shortest time possible. Basketball is a series of sprints, rather than a continuous running. According to experiments made, a player is in action less than 40% of the actual playing time. But he must move at a maximum speed to get there before the other player. This entails quick starting, and rapid movement, with the body in perfect control, as he may need to change his course to avoid another player who comes at any angle into his path.

9. Self-confidence—Each player must be able to carry on by himself if necessary. There are times when he cannot depend on his team mates to do even the things that they are better qualified for than himself, but he must perform of himself. He must be, to the greatest extent possible, an all round performer.

10. Self-sacrifice—In basketball there is no place for the egotist or for the one who is not willing to let another have all the credit if that will further the game. The unit in basketball is the team, not the individual player, and the one who would try to get glory at the sacrifice of the game is a hindrance to the team. These two in their proper place, though apparently contradictory, depend on the judgment of the player as to which he will do.

11. Self-control—He must be able to subordinate his feelings to his reflexes as any interference will interrupt the proper performance of his skill and he will be unable to do his best work. The one who permits his feelings to interfere is not only a hindrance to his team, but he is occupying the place of another man who would do this. There are so few players on a team that one player not doing his best is a greater reduction in the relative strength of the team than in some games where the ratio is less.

12. Sportsmanship—On account of the proximity of the spectators to the players and that fact that they can observe not only every movement, but also every player, he must observe the rules of the game. The officials must be impartial and competent to retain the respect of the crowd, and to keep the game under control. The players have found out that it pays to observe the rules and accept the decision of the officials.

PRELIMINARY TRAINING FOR BASKETBALL

Athletic training consists of three main factors: first, the development of the necessary reflexes to make a skillful player; second, the development of the structure and the functions of the body that it may be capable of standing the strain and recover from extra effort; and third, a proper attention to the nervous system just previous to, and during a game, that he may operate at his highest efficiency.

The lack of any one of these will greatly handicap any team. Most coaches realize the necessity of the first, and many endeavor to make use of the factors which assist the third, but neglect almost entirely the second. No amount of enthusiasm will fully compensate for the lack of the physique or skill.

Some coaches plead with the spectators to stimulate the players by cheering and a show of confidence. This is good when the other factors have been developed, but is worse than useless when they have been neglected. Outside stimulation interferes with half formed reflexes, and it may overstimulate the player who has more emotion than his physical nature can stand.

Basketball is preeminently a game of skill, and this requires a long period of practice to become proficient. Skill is complex and is made up of simpler factors, the fundamental one of which is **muscular control**. Muscular control is the proper amount of stimulation given to the proper muscles or group of muscles, at the proper time and to the proper amount. Several of these muscle controls when united form a co-ordination, and when several co-ordinations are untied we get a reflex and when several reflexes follow each other we get skill.

It is impossible to acquire skill while the mind is distracted with a number of details. By developing a number of these fundamental factors one at a time the whole skill is readily acquired. The fundamentals that are needed are:

1. To receive the ball in such a way that it remains in the hand or hands. **The eye must be trained so that the hand will be in the proper place to receive the ball.** The hand must be so sensitized that the instant the ball touches it the fingers will close with the proper tension. The arms must begin to ease the shock by giving way so as to stop the ball by degrees rather than abruptly. This is the method employed in lacrosse or in tennis when catching the ball on the racket. The individual who can secure the ball is only partly trained as he must use the ball after he has gotten it.

2. To be able to **deliver the ball** so as to accomplish the act desired requires that the player learn all the different ways of passing the ball and the best method to use under the varying

conditions. Most coaches who have written on the game go into detail on these subjects.

3. When and how to dribble—There has been much antagonism to the dribble in basketball, but it is an essential part of the game, not to make it an aggressive part of the offense, as it should be used to get away from an opponent, or to get into a position to make a pass or shot. This phase of the game requires more practice than almost any other phase and it demands a higher degree of skill than any other, consequently should form a part of the preliminary training.

4. Shooting for goal—This is the most essential part of the game as it depends on the winning of the game. The basketball goal was set horizontal rather than upright because in an indoor game it was essential to stress skill rather than speed or drive, as the latter made for roughness.

The ball must be thrown not directly at the goal, but elevated in such a way as to fall into the opening. Because of this the point at which the ball is aimed varies with the distance from the goal and the height from which it is delivered. Not only must the direction be controlled but the force given to the ball must be suited to the conditions. These factors must be acquired by practice as no definite rules can be given to suit all conditions. This skill can be acquired by practice. One of the earliest ever-victorious teams worked under very serious handicaps. They could practice only twice per week, but the players, who could get there, practiced goal shooting from every angle at every opportunity. Out of the twenty-nine games played they won every one of them. The highest score was 72; the lowest, 8; the average was 35; and the total score of points was 1052 to their opponents 203, making five points for every one of their opponents.

5. The ability of the individual to co-operate in such a way with the other members of the team that the ball may be passed to a player so that there will be no lost motion, no slowing up

to wait for the ball, nor reaching to catch a ball that has been thrown too far ahead of a running player. This can best be acquired by having the team go on the floor and pass the ball from one to another while they are in full motion and dodging out and in. Progress can be made by permitting an opponent to attempt to get the ball, then adding another until four men are opposed to five and the five are able to keep the ball indefinitely. In the games played before the British army the officers thought that they could easily learn the game and getting out on the floor they found that they could not get their hands on the ball. It looked so easy and was done so gracefully by the Americans that they thought it easy. The fact is that it requires a great deal of practice. Most players want to get into actual games and are unwilling to spend time on the essentials.

When these essentials have been mastered it is easy to develop teamwork and to get the players to co-operate.

THE OFFENSE IN BASKETBALL

Theoretically there is neither offense or defense in basketball, as any man has a right to get the ball whenever he can. In this respect basketball differs from football, baseball, tennis, and resembles such games as soccer, lacrosse, and hockey, in which the ball may change hands at any time. In basketball, where running with the ball is prohibited, the possession of the ball depends on the skill of the player to pass the ball to his teammates in such a way that they can receive it without interference from the opponents.

Most of the teams which have made phenomenal success in winning games or championships have done so by stressing the offense. The coach of the "Wonder Team" of Passaic states that he has stressed the offense almost to the neglect of the defense. The 23rd St. Y. M. C. A. team with 29 victories in one season did little but practice offense.

In basketball the offense consists of passing the ball from one member of the team to another in such a way as to retain possession of it. The fundamentals of the offense are:

Handling the Ball

To make a successful offense it is necessary to be able to catch the ball in any position of the catcher or in any direction of the pass. It is impossible in every case for the passer to do what he would like to do and the catcher must assist him.

Passing the Ball

1. The passer must pass the ball in such a manner that the catcher can get the ball safely into his hands, and retain it. It should be passed directly and without curve or wobble.
2. It should be passed so that the catcher can get to the point of advantage without a break in his movement—not too far ahead or so far ahead that he will need to reach, nor so close that he will need to stop or slow up.
3. It should reach him in such a way that he will be ready to make his next move without changing his position. If he is near and about to shoot for goal, it should be so high that he will not need to stoop but can deliver it.
4. It should be passed with little danger of being intercepted by an opponent. It is not uncommon to see a passed ball caught by one of the opponents because the passer did not judge his position and ability.
5. He should conceal as far as possible the direction of his pass. This may be done by looking, by a movement of the eyes, or by a feint of the hands or body. The opponent will endeavor to anticipate your movement and if you can get him to plan to intercept one movement, and you execute another, you will have a double start on him as he must break his first reflex and begin another. Few seem to realize the importance of a split second in a movement. Basketball players, as a group, have the best sight and touch reaction among the athletes.
6. Dribble or pass in such a way as to attract the attention of two of the opponents even momentarily, thus giving a player the

start. This may be done by coming between them so that they hesitate as to which shall take the approaching player.

The Players without the Ball

1. Just as the man with the ball can feint and attempt to confuse the opponents, so the others can feint as to where they are going—keep their opponents guessing. In a zone of defense he must not go out of the zone until the opponent has been drawn where he wants him. If he strikes for another part of the field, his opponent will return in time to check the player.
2. As many players as possible should be free and near at the time the player wants to deliver the ball. With several free to obtain the ball, the thrower becomes a triple threat man and more deceiving.
3. The team with the ball should vary the attack so that the opponents will not anticipate their movements.

THE USE OF BASKETBALL IN CORRECTIVE WORK

Corrective work means any form of motor activity that will correct deformities of any kind in the human mechanism, be it structural or functional. Many physical directors also use it as meaning any form of gymnastics that is done in class work and confounds it with development work.

To what extent can basketball be used for this type of work? First, it may be used to correct several kinds of **deformities**. It is especially helpful in correcting **abnormalities of unused nerves** such as those conditions produced by infantile paralysis, where the habit has been formed of using the normal limb and neglecting to use the affected side. Not many years ago it was thought impossible to restore a muscle in which the nerve had been atrophied and no effort was made to assist it to recover and more and more it continued to atrophy and contract until the arm was drawn across the body and rotated inwards and the fingers closed by the shortening of the flexor muscles which are stronger than the extensor. A paper read before a medical society fifteen years ago brought out much criticism by the society. Even the magazines took it up and suggested that it might be advisable to read some former papers which maintained that a nerve once gone could never be restored. Which is perfectly true, but the question arose, "when is a nerve degenerated completely so that it will not respond to treatment?"

A student came into my office to get exemption from the required exercise and on being told that exercise might greatly help him, he became interested at once and inquired what he could do to help his condition. It was suggested that he might play basketball. He immediately answered that he could not get around on his lame leg nor handle the ball with his lame arm. When he found that he could play with the ball, shooting goals and playing by himself, he began a systematic course of corrective work, coming out every day and playing by himself, making the lame leg carry him and using the lame arm in throwing the ball. Inside of two weeks he could notice the benefit and was encouraged to keep the work up. Before leaving college he was able to play with other players in a friendly game and his walk had been so much improved that his parents took the trouble to find out what was making this change, and on being told that it was basketball, they were surprised and delighted.

Basketball is one game that individuals will work at for hours at a time without competition of other players. There is an interest in trying to make goals not only for those who wish to perfect themselves, but also those who want activity for recreation or pleasure. It is valuable where activity is needed but the extreme forms prohibited.

Basketball is excellent to improve posture as it strengthens the muscles of the back, and especially those of the upper shoulders and neck. You need only watch an expert player running with the ball and tossing it as he leaps up to place it in the basket. This same exercise strengthens the abdominal muscles whenever the trunk is thrown back of the perpendicular. When the ball is tossed from the chest or lower, the muscles that pull the trunk upright are developed and when the motion is continued it straightens out the spine. Throwing the ball from over head strengthens the muscles that pull the upper part of the trunk forward and develops the abdomen.

Basketball is good for any person who is clumsy and will not mix with other persons because of this. As soon as they become interested by practicing alone they will begin to play the game with others.

It is a good game to reduce as it demands stooping, raising the body, running and jumping. Begin slowly and keep the body active.

The method of operation is: set up a number of goals and give each group a ball and they will work away at that exercise without the constant attendance of the instructor. These goals do not require a high ceiling as they are carried on at close range, and several groups may be working at the same time in a small space.

BASKETBALL IN CLASS WORK

In most of our colleges basketball, along with other games, has been used as an intercollegiate sport and some few have been made expert. It has interested the whole school in the game. It has been used as a means of advertising the institution but little thought has been given to the benefit to the players, much less to the student body as a whole.

Lately there has been a clamor for intramural basketball, and it is used in this way in most of the colleges today. The endeavor is to make athletics more extensive in the institutions. This has been done by making the competition between organizations and has been helpful in getting a great many interested in athletics.

Basketball has not yet found its place in a system of physical education, whereas it is splendidly adapted for many of the best factors. It is not a whole system in itself, but could play an integral part in its place. This is especially true of college work where there is a greater uniformity in growth than there is in the secondary schools.

A method we employed at the University of Kansas worked so well that it may solve some of the difficulties. Physical exercise is required of the freshmen and sophomores. The aim of the department was to give every student an opportunity to get the benefits of the different forms of gymnastics and games. For this purpose the season was arranged so that the student would get the greatest use of the equipment. Instead of making the season for basketball correspond with that of the competition in intercollegiate, we arranged the season so that the basketball for class work came in that season when the basketball courts were not occupied. This was in the first quarter when the coaches were interested in football and could not give their time to basketball, leaving the courts open most of the day. The regular classes were at ten, eleven, three, four and five, making five and sometimes six classes. Each class formed a group and was so treated.

Within each of these groups teams were formed and a regular schedule was played. These teams were selected, not according to the regulation plan, but with the end of getting the greatest benefit to the greatest number. The class was lined up alphabetically. Then all those who had played tournament basketball were asked to step six paces forward, then all those who had played, but not on a regular team, were asked to take three paces forward. This left three groups. The usual way is to make up teams within these groups. Instead of this, all were given "right dress" and there were three lines of different experience; those who had been experts, those who had had a little, and those who had never played basketball. Curiously enough, in Kansas these groups were almost equal in numbers. Instead of dividing the groups up into teams as usual, we divided the whole group up by making the team consist of two experts, two players and two who had never played. This was done with the idea that the more expert would help the less expert. One of the advance players was made captain and the other manager and the team was turned over to them as a team.

There was a basket for each team so that they could do their practicing of the fundamentals as a team. Then when the time came for the contest, eight teams were put on the double court. A time keeper was given a gong which he was to ring every five minutes. Four teams played while the other four teams were watching and planning their game. From the time the gong sounded until the next four teams took the floor was five seconds, and then the ball was thrown up for the next game. Not once during the whole season was it necessary to halt the game for the players to be in their position or to throw it up when only one team was in position.

Several factors showed the advantages of this:

1. At the end of the quarter it was impossible to pick out the players who had been in the inexperienced row as they had been developed by their team mates.
2. The manager and captain had experience in coaching and managing.
3. The freshman coach stood in the gallery and could pick out the players who looked as if they would make available material for the higher specialization. Some of these were not from the first group; some were even from the third.

The best team of each class entered a tournament to decide the winners. The schedule was carried out with 56 teams, enjoyed by all and no prizes given.

BASKETBALL FOR HIGH SCHOOL BOYS

There are several factors in the growth of the high school boy that necessitates special care in its use; first, the boys are of different stages of growth and maturity and for this reason the class is usually composed of boys of different development. There are boys who are short, and some tall, some matured for their age, some light and undeveloped, and some heavy. For this reason it is hard to get any game that they can all play together, especially where there is personal contact, as the light and the immature stand little show with their more developed mates. Such games as football and soccer and baseball are even less adapted for these persons. The main difficulty lies in getting competition between teams. To keep up the interest as the skill of the individual increases it is necessary to give them some contests. The student will work better if there is a project before him in this matter as well as in other affairs. If any game is beneficial to the student, one is as much entitled to the benefit as another, and if it is an educational factor, then each should not only get an opportunity to play the game, but it should be made a part his education.

Basketball, on account of its intrinsic interest to boys, has very frequently been abused, especially by high school coaches. Some call the roll, throw out a basketball or two and let the students regulate the game to suit themselves and play as they please. There is little wonder that the bigger boys select the teams and exclude the less able ones and make them sit on the side lines while they get the benefits of the game; the others getting a chance only when the bigger ones have tired out.

Another plan is to **modify the rules so that all manner of personal contact is allowed** and the student can do anything he pleases with the ball or the opponent so long as they do not get angry and fight or attempt to injure the other player. This is a good way to develop the larger groups of muscles which is a necessary part of the training of the youth, but it spoils the game. It would be easy to make rules that would so modify the game that it might include this factor, but it is no longer basketball, but more resembles English rugby, which might well be introduced into the school system as an outdoor sport. Basketball is personal combat without personal contact.

Basketball was adapted for the purpose of eliminating roughness and developing the power of accomplishing the purpose without personal contact while occupying the same floor, differing from volleyball and tennis, where the opponents have no opportunity for personal contact. In basketball there is needed that restraint which is eliminated when we use the game in the manner suggested above. Basketball in high school should be kept in its proper place and used for its own special use.

The director can divide up his class into teams and have them play a regular schedule at the close of the period, instead of occupying the whole time in contest. A number of baskets may be hung around the court and the teams spend some time in throwing baskets, dribbling and passing, thus each individual gets the benefit of the game and is interested in it.

In selecting the teams there are two general principles to follow: Select your teams in such a way that each team can compete against each other. This can be done by selecting some large boys and some smaller on each team and the team can adjust itself to the other team's style of play. If the object of the game is educational, there is no reason why the director may not place the players of each team so that the least objection arises from these conditions.

A large part of each period should be taken up with the development of the fundamentals so that when the opportunity for more extended competition arises, the student will be prepared, and he will receive a greater amount of pleasure and satisfaction from the game.

The game should be used as an educational factor rather than as a method of making compulsory Physical Education easy for the Director.

BASKETBALL FOR GRADE SCHOOL BOYS

I am very frequently asked the question as to whether basketball is a suitable game for grade school age. In order to answer this question intelligently it is necessary to know what the purpose of physical education is for this group, and also how this purpose is best accomplished. Boys of this age differ from mature men in that exercise should influence this development, then it is necessary to adjust the form to the requirements. While those who have reached maturity need, not so much development, as recreation.

The grade school boy needs muscular development and should have the kind of work that will develop that attribute. At the same time he should also be acquiring skills that will form a useful part of his physical equipment. Basketball may well, then, be a part of the work of the grade school and a very useful part, as it develops many of the most valuable attributes.

However, there is no necessity for the boy to be made to work with the man's equipment—it might well be modified to suit the child. It is harassing to watch a grade school boy try to throw goals when he cannot throw for the goal with ease and some degree of accuracy.

By lowering the goal to his needs his accuracy and his interest will both be increased.

In this stage of development the competition between rooms or other organizations should be limited as the good effects of development of skill is often neutralized by the effort to accomplish some object which interferes with the practice of some skill that has been newly acquired. If the games are short, and the rivalry is not too intense, then the skill already acquired will be used and become more valuable. Each practice should be mainly in the nature of acquiring new skills and a brief game at the conclusion of the drill will be valuable to increase the interest and enthusiasm of the boys in athletic activity.

At this age it is necessary to closely **observe the players** and adapt their positions on the floor to the nervous development of the boy. Some boys naturally take to competition and excel at it while others have neither the interest nor the skill to play the game in the same way. The latter should be encouraged by giving them **special instruction** in the fundamentals, and they should not be discouraged by scolding or pointing out their weaknesses but take it for granted that they are making progress, and encourage them to keep on with the fundamentals.

If basketball is an aid to the development of the individual then it should be given to **those who lack, rather than those who excel**. It is not necessary then, to keep the expert back, but it is essential that all the class get the benefit of the sport.

Interschool games are useful to add zest to the game, but if it is necessary to slight some of the students, it is better to slight those who are already expert.

In grade school the necessity for **advertising** the institution is of **very minor importance** as the children are compelled to attend in most places and there is not a need to increase the number of students. In many communities the choice of which school he shall attend is settled by the superintendent, and not by the choice of the individual. While it may be advantageous to advertise the teacher or the principal, yet this should not interfere with the welfare of the child. It is well to keep in mind all the time that **the purpose of all the school activities is for the pupil.**

BASKETBALL IN RURAL SCHOOLS

I have been asked to start a propaganda against the use of basketball in rural schools, not by students, parents, teachers, or school superintendents, but by a state superintendent of instruction. His objections against the game were that there was not enough of any one age or sex to give good competition and in some cases the girls had to play with or against the boys to make up the team.

Personally, I believe that basketball is especially adapted for Rural Schools. Children brought up on a farm or in the suburbs usually have done enough physical work to give them a good physique and they do not need the kind of exercise that will develop strong muscles. The kind of exercise that will be best for them is that which will give extension rather than contraction and will loosen up the whole muscular system and will use the muscles that are frequently left out in other forms of mechanical or agricultural work. It will give physical judgment, and especially will it give co-operation between the players. We hear so frequently that farmers will not co-operate. The work on a farm is largely individual and it soon becomes a habit and the person not only depends on himself, but even distrusts the ability of other people, and perhaps their intentions.

In playing basketball one of the most needed attributes is co-operation. He learns to work with others, to depend on their assistance, to give and take and enjoy his association and co-operation which soon become a habit and he has begun a much needed course of conduct. Basketball is peculiarly adapted to conditions of this kind. It is interesting enough for the student to play for long periods, trying to make goals and thus increasing accuracy and smoothness of movement resulting in graceful poise of the body. By arranging a series of goals, as many as needed, and giving each group a ball and goal, it is easy to get competition between dissimilar groups. By a system of handicapping, the large boys can be made equal to the smaller, the smaller girls can be equalized with the larger girls, and competition can be carried on and the pupils get the benefit of the game. One of the group gets into the best position for him to make a goal and it is the business of the others to get the ball to him in the quickest possible manner so that he may take his shot, then make room for the next pupil. Thus they shoot in turn and each gets the benefit of the game. By counting the number of goals made in a certain time it is possible to have competitions and yet avoid all the supposed objections. If the school is divided up into teams and the team equalized by having the bigger boys make five to three of the little ones' goals, they will all work as hard as if they were all of the same size. The actual handicapping would be a matter of experience and trial.

One difficulty is that when the larger pupils want the ball the smaller ones want it at the same time. The best way is to give each group a ball of their own and give them a personal interest in keeping it in good shape, not permitting the larger boys to use it if their own ball is not in condition. Make the careless team suffer for its own carelessness. Thus we teach them a needed lesson and satisfy the feeling of justice in the minds of those who work to keep their equipment in good condition.

Too many look on athletics as either a method of competition or a means of recreation, not as one of the implements of genuine education. Accuracy can be obtained in basketball as well as in mathematics, and will be used in the use of the body as well as the other in use of the mind. Grace of movement, easy control of body, are valuable assets not only in the school room, but all through life. The teacher who is interested in making the boys and girls the best men and women that it is possible for them to become will adapt the games to this end and will be a success as a teacher.

BASKETBALL AND THE CHURCHES

Basketball was devised for the Departments of Physical Education, but it was not long until the churches saw its possibilities and Dr. Halls Church, of New York City, had a team in October, 1897, when they played a game with the 23rd St. Y. M. C. A. Since that time the church has made use of basketball.

The first church to have a regular schedule was the First M. E. Church of North Hampton, which was a schedule of 28 games in 1902. In 1904 there was formed a church league in New York City and the year following a league was formed in Cleveland. In 1909 a Sunday School league was formed in Kansas City and since that time it has been used extensively. Many churches have a gymnasium where practice is held and games are played.

The churches and Sunday Schools first used it as a drawing card for their classes. Watching a game between one of the largest Sunday School classes and an industrial team, I asked the teacher who was present if he considered it consistent for a Sunday School teacher to encourage his class in playing such a game. He immediately said, "Man alive, do you not know that it is one of the factors that helps to hold my class together?"

A good illustration of the effect of basketball was given me by an official in answer to the question if the players on a Sunday School team were good sportsmen. He answered in this way, "There are some boys who play on a Sunday School team and also on an industrial team." On being asked, he said that these same men played much cleaner ball when they were playing with the Sunday School team than when they were playing with the other team.

A classmate in college, writing of the work done by the class members, after mentioning some who were high in church work, some were missionaries, after recounting their work, said that after all, perhaps none of them had made a more lasting contribution to the humanity than the one who introduced basketball, not because there was any great benefit in the game itself, but because it gave the churches and Sunday Schools a tool with which to work. Churches are today putting gymnasiums in their buildings and they are considered a useful adjunct to its equipment.

BASKETBALL IN INDUSTRIAL INSTITUTIONS

Physical activities in industrial institutions is different from that used in colleges. The educational value is of less interest because the participants are more or less mature and do not need muscular development. Their work is more or less monotonous and thereby dulls the emotions. The use of their leisure time is an important factor in the development of their character and this reflects on the kind of work they do. "Our living is made in our working hours, but our character is made in our leisure time." Many of our industrial institutions appreciate the value of the proper use of their spare time and provide facilities. This should take the form of activities that will be interesting and active.

Basketball was intended for just such conditions. It originated in an institution devoted to the care of young men who were more or less mature and did not need the development of the muscular system, but did need recreation to offset the conditions of the working day.

1. It was intended mainly as a recreative sport where the association of others was on a level of democracy. Even in the army the officers and privates met in an equality on the basketball court and the give and take of the court was beneficial to both. This does not make for insubordination, but the man in control who can play the game as man to man gains the respect of those whom he directs and they will follow him in his desires.

2. The development of the reflexes makes a man more capable. It makes their hands and fingers more dexterous and their bodies more agile. It puts into use muscles and groups that may have lain idle for years. Basketball is preeminently a game of skill where brute strength counts for little, where the maximum contest is found with the minimum of personal contact. These factors are carried over into their everyday work.

3. It gives the individual something to think about when the reflex activities are at work and the mind must be active in some way. His mind is active in thinking of the game rather than in brooding over some supposed inequality or slight that he may have.

4. It develops loyalty to the institutions. Most workers look upon the organization for which they work as a source of income which should be obtained with the minimum of effort; but

when they begin to fight for their institution and give of their time and efforts for that institution they are going to give their best for its advancement. The colleges retain the amateur status in their athletes because they know that working for the honor of the institution brings better results in the student body than working for pay.

Basketball can be used to greater advantage than most other team games.

1. Because it is played in the evening and thus does not interfere with the working hours.
2. It is inexpensive, the equipment in use outside of the field and the goals is very little.
3. The team is small and a few men can get together when a large number would find it difficult to get away at the same time. A large number of small teams has as much advantage if not more than a large number of individuals playing the same game.
4. It is not necessary for the players to return to the plant unless they so desire, as they can organize a team and play with outside leagues, but the equipment may be supplied by the organization. This gives the maximum benefits with the minimum of expense and effort.
5. Basketball is the most universally played game, consequently there are more opportunities than in any other game.
6. It is not necessary to get expert players to get the benefits of the game. A representative team may advertise the institution, but a team of raw members playing under the auspices of the institution gets the benefits individually and this reacts on their work and their attitude toward the institution.

BASKETBALL FOR GIRLS

In the spring of 1892 a group of girls came to me and asked if basketball was not a good game for girls. They were school teachers and had been watching the boys play until they were imbued with the idea that they too would enjoy the sport. My answer at that time was that I could see no reason why girls could not play the game. Of course basketball was not the scientific game that it is at present—the floor was small and the players were more inclined to keep their positions on the floor. When the game became more specialized and the floors were enlarged the question again arose as to the **fitness of the game for girls**. Many girls played with boys' rules and as the game increased in speed basketball was denounced as a sport unfit for girls. The division of the court into three areas was then introduced and the running from one end of the field to another was eliminated. Smith's College was one of the first women's colleges to take up the game, and in 1894 Leland Stanford played the girls of the University of California.

Basketball as a game has been a wonderful help to the girls of the community as it has been the only game where there was an opportunity for personal contact with an elimination of the running phase of the game. The girls who played basketball began to get a good idea of sportsmanship. I have seen games in which girl players slapped each other and did not wait for the decision of the referee to put them off the floor but ran off the field as soon as they became conscious of what they reflexly had done. It is needless to say that the offense was not repeated by that player. Basketball has enabled the girls to get an opportunity to develop and to display good sportsmanship.

There was a time when there was some doubt as to the effect basketball might have on the **aesthetic side** of the girls' nature, but this has been put aside as so many teams of girls have illustrated that it does not destroy their lady's instincts. The Old Grads of Edmonton ought to show this if there was any change taking place in the temperament of the girls, as that team raised $11,000 and took a trip through most of the countries of Europe, playing every team with whom they could schedule a game and winning them all, yet these girls were perfect ladies in the drawing rooms as well as on the basketball court. **Sportsmanship is not a natural instinct** but is acquired only through being brought to the attention of the person and there is no more forcible way of impressing this attribute on a person than by inflicting punishment on the player for infringement of the rules. This leads them to weigh the consequences and to select the most worthy course. This teaches them to get the proper perspective between the emotions near at hand and those lying in the future. I have no fear that basketball, or any other game where restraint is demanded of the player, contains any danger of the players becoming rough or indifferent to the rights of others. So often we hear that you cannot **legislate sportsmanship** into an individual. While this may be true, it is just as certain that we can, by enforcing the rules, cause a **habit of morality** or the sticking to a standard, which is morality, and the one who observes the rules of a community will be considered as moral.

Basketball, if properly administered as to players, time of play, regard for the rules, and a proper attention to the hygenic conditions is an **excellent recreation for girls**. It has been my good fortune to attend banquets given for the players in a basketball league and it was an inspiring sight to see a large group of girls who in a large city could find recreation and enjoyment during their leisure hours enjoying a game that was helpful to them physically, reflexly and even morally.

Basketball for girls may be made as interesting and more beneficial than the movies, the dancehalls or even bridge, and as it can be played in the evening it does not take away from the duties of the working day. Much more might be gotten from basketball for girls in industrial institutions if conditions were made more attractive and opportunities given for engaging in such sports. It would give a healthy tone to body and mind.

Basketball is not something that must be enforced on the group as they instinctively take to the game and most of the trouble in many institutions comes from the playing of basketball to the exclusion of other activities because it is intrinsically interesting.

I do not think that the present girl's rules are the best from the standpoint of the players. On account of the restraining lines some of the players never get a chance to act on the offense but are limited to the negative or obstructive side, and may form a habit of being knockers rather than boosters. To remedy this it would only require that the floor be divided into two areas and that the position of the players be changed at half time, thus giving each an equal chance to obtain all the benefits of the game.

THE EVOLUTION OF THE BALL

That there must be a ball of some kind was the first factor settled in making the game of basketball. All of the so-called team games have a ball of some kind, or something that takes the place of a ball. One of the requirements of the game we sought was that it should be easy to learn, so that men who had had little experience in athletics could get the benefit of the game. Most of the games played with a small ball require some kind of an intermediate apparatus, such as tennis, hockey, lacrosse, etc. This makes the game more difficult to learn. A large ball is handled by the hands and requires little practice to be able to begin playing. There were two large balls in use at that time. The Rugby football was large and oblate in form and especially adapted for carrying it in the arms, but was not so valuable when carrying the ball was prohibited. The Soccer ball was round and the same in all directions, and was more easily handled with the hands. It could be handled in any position and could be thrown, batted or bounced with greater accuracy. Consequently, it was chosen as the best adapted for the purpose.

The first rule book specified that "the ball shall be an ordinary Association football." The goals were then fifteen inches in diameter. The first change made in the ball was in 1895–96, where the rule reads: Rule II, Section 1. "The ball shall be round; it shall be made of a rubber bladder covered with a leather case; it shall be not less than 30, nor more than 32 inches in circumference."

Sec. 3. The ball made by the Overman Wheel Company shall be the official ball.

Sec. 4. The official ball must be used in all match games.

In 1897 another clause was added. Rule II, Section 1. The limit of variableness shall be not more than one-fourth of an inch in three diameters. It shall weight not less than 18 nor more than 20 ounces.

Sec. 4. The official ball shall be used in all match games.

In 1903: Rule II, Sec. 4. The official ball must be used in all match games. The Referee may, in all match games, and shall, in all serial championships, declare all games void where this rule is violated.

Sec. 4. The official ball must be used in all league games and by all affiliated teams.

In the first issue of the Collegiate rules, 1905–06, this rule concerning the official ball is inserted as a footnote. From that time, the choice of the ball has been left in the hands of the conferences or teams. This has led to a marked improvement in the ball.

In 1909 the manufacturers maintained that a ball of the specified weight could not be made to stand the strain to which they were subjected and the weight of the ball was increased from 18–20 ounces to 20–23 ounces. Official size and weight of official balls are now as follows: Shall measure not less than 30, nor more than 31 inches in circumference and shall weigh not less than 20 nor more than 22 ounces.

Rawlings Official Balls conform to these rules.

When the different makers of balls all met these requirements the makers began to introduce certain refinements. At first the quality of the material and the way in which it kept its shape were the main points of attention. Later refinements resulted in changes in the structure of the ball. The early balls were all made with the lacing and the stem valve on the same side of the ball, and this resulted in a lopsided ball, one side being heavier than the others. As the skill of the players increased and the competition became keener, there was an attempt to counterpoise the ball. This was effected mainly by the introduction of the outside valve inserted in the side opposite to the lacing, which divided the weight. It also made it easier to keep the ball inflated to the proper pressure, thus eliminating the element of the chance which always favors the unskilled team. The weight of the lacing was reduced as much as possible and an approximation to balance was acquired. The latest achievement is found where the lacing is invisible and a true balance established, so that it rolls, bounces, or rests at any position.

The Rawlings No. AXL Official Concealed Lace Basketball, I believe, is a decided advance in basketball construction.

No. AXS Rawlings-Naismith Official Crossed Lace Valve Type Inter-collegiate Basketball. Made in four sections of the finest cuts from extra selected pebble grain steer hides, tanned especially for Rawlings, from which the stretch is eliminated. The special double lining will absolutely keep the ball in perfect shape. The crossed lace holds opening in ball tightly closed and prevents bulging at this point. Sewed throughout with finest waxed linen thread. Improved valve construction permits of **inflation and deflation without disturbing the lace**. A standard air pressure can be maintained and accurately gauged by air gauge. **A feature** of this ball is that bladder can be replaced without returning ball to factory and a special designed valve nut that cannot turn or pull out.

Packed complete **already Laced**, with pure gum stemless bladder, inflating auxiliaries and patented lacing needle, in sealed box.

Office Size, Shape and Weight

No. AXL Rawlings-Naismith Official Concealed Lace Valve Type Inter-collegiate Basketball. Construction and materials in this ball are the same as in our No. AXS Naismith ball, with the exception of the concealed lacing feature.

The lacing feature in our No. AXL brings the two edges of the ball opening tightly together without bulge or gaping and they stay there. The lace itself is not subject to wear and relacing is reduced to a minimum even after a season's play. If relacing ever should become necessary, the No. AXL can be relaced quickly and simply with the special lacing needle furnished and it is if anything even simpler to replace a bladder in the No. AXL ball than in a regularly laced ball. Packed complete **already laced** with pure gum stemless bladder, inflating auxiliaries, special lacing needle, lacing instructions, in sealed box.

Valve nut cannot turn or pull out

Official Size, Shape and Weight

Basketballs No. AXS and AXL have been designed by party whose name they bear or by Rawlings Mfg. Co. in collaboration with that party.

Basketball's Place in the
Physical Education Program

Radio Program, January 6, 1938

A radio interview conducted between Dr. Forrest "Phog" Allen and James Naismith. Conducted on January 6, 1938, the program is entitled "Basketball's Place in the Physical Education Program."

ALLEN: Dr. Naismith, we have chosen for our subject of discussion tonight "Basketball's Place in the Physical Education Program". Since you originated basketball and since you were trained in the pioneer school of physical education, namely Springfield, Mass. Y.M.C.A. College, it seems to me that this subject is an especially fitting one on which you can speak authoritatively. Do you think, Dr. Naismith, there is a danger of the physical educator today neglecting the body-building part of physical education and depending entirely on games for a system of physical education? This, of course, has reference to basketball as well as some of the other games.

NAISMITH: Absolutely yes! A great many of our physical educators are looking at it from the standpoint of the interest of the authorities and of spectators, rather than of benefit that can come to the boy, and a good many of these physical educators have been brought up and have received their appointments largely because of their ability in playing games rather than in their technical knowledge of the development of manhood.

ALLEN: Dr. Naismith, I find myself agreeing with you very emphatically in this statement. However, I can also see how an expert in the games would have a basic knowledge of a particular sport. This exceptional knowledge and splendid skill that he has developed in the sport is only symptomatic of his interest in the larger program of play and physical education. Most of these coaches who are now teaching physical education undoubtedly had a basic yearning for play in physical education. This, of course, caused them to continue their study to the point where they specialized in their life's work.

NAISMITH: Dr. Allen, don't think for a moment that I do not appreciate the skill that these boys get in learning a game and in devoting their time to it,—Both the fundamentals and the mechanism of the game; but I do lament the ignorance of a lot of our directors of physical education in the real science of developing the boy into a man. Take, for instance, a man who had been appointed to head the physical education in a city of 80,000, who came to me and told me he didn't know a single thing about anything but football and basketball, and he wondered if I could help him out in making out a program. It is the employment by principals of men of this type that has practically done away with the real physical education program. I was very glad, as I visited your gymnasium the other morning, Dr. Allen, to see the large class of majors who are beginning at the bottom and learning the gymnastic side as well as the recreative side of the development of the body. Now you are developing the men who are going out to head departments of physical education. Is your program, as it is arranged at the present time, comprehensive so as to include all those different parts?

ALLEN: Well, Doctor, we are not sure about that, but we are definitely endeavoring to find out. By asking men of your caliber who certainly know physical education, and then by doing a job analysis program, as Dean W. W. Chartors would call it, we are endeavoring to find out from superintendents and principals in the state of Kansas just what is needed for this state. We are asking those questions and when the survey is completed we believe we will know.

NAISMITH: Why do you go to superintendents and principals and ask them? Why don't you tell them? For instance, a year or so ago a man told me— "I have looked this thing over, spent 30 minutes studying the set-up." And I returned, "I have spent 30 years studying this situation, and yet you think you know more about it than I do."

ALLEN: Well, Dr. Naismith, you really put me right on the grill, and I like this. I don't mean that we are going to shape our course exactly like all those fellows would suggest, but we want to know what they think are the needs for the schools of this state. Then we are contacting physical educators like Dr. Thomas Storoy of Stanford, Dr. Jesse F. Williams and Dr. Fritz Maroney of Columbia University, Dr. J. B. Nash of New York University, Floyd Rowe who is an authority and has charge of physical education for the public schools of Cleveland, Ohio, Dr. Anderson of St. Louis, and then of course we are cooperating with our cousins here in Kansas—Professor L. P. Washburn of Kansas State College, and Coffman of Washburn College, with a view of having an all-round program that will fill the needs of the high schools of the State of Kansas.

NAISMITH: Doctor, you have mentioned a lot of men, and very prominent men. Can you tell me this: In my early days almost every man who was a director of physical education was an M.D. Today there are only two of those you mentioned who are M.D.'s, and they are old standbys. Now, why is it that physical education has gone from the medical profession to the educational?

ALLEN: That is a very excellent point, Dr. Naismith. The only answer that I could give that seems logical would be that the men with an M.D. degree can earn very much more than the professor of physical education. The health program of the country has called the doctors of medicine, and then, too, there has been such an expansion of the physical education program that the colleges have established a curriculum for physical education majors. That curriculum calls for a study of the basic sciences, and most of these physical education majors that are going out now have passed satisfactorily courses in anatomy, physiology, biology and chemistry. Of course, it would be fine if they could have a medical background, but that would require a much longer course than a four-year college course.

NAISMITH: Then you consider there is a trend backward to a study of the operations of the body, and that it is a necessity that they understand part of the human body in order to develop a real physical education program.

ALLEN: By all means, Dr. Naismith. I do not see how any intelligent physical education director or athletic coach can do a good job unless he definitely understands the structure and functions of the human body. Diet, fatigue, training, as well as fundamental body building, must of necessity be understood by this individual before he can do justice to the boy. And do not forget this point—a coach who has never had a course in psychology will not have the best understanding of his subject—the boy.

NAISMITH: Doctor, I would like to ask you one question. Do you know, or do you think there is a high school superintendent or principal who wouldn't accept "Whizzor" White as head of a department of physical education, even if he never had a day's study of physiology, or anything of that kind?

ALLEN: Well, Doctor, you are hitting me right in the middle. I believe most of them would take him. And there is a weakness there. But you brought up the name of a wonderful young man who perhaps is not trained in physical education and maybe wouldn't take the job. We both know that he is a Phi Beta Kappa and has been selected as a Rhodes Scholar from Colorado. They tell me that he is about everything that you would want in a young college graduate. Don't you think if "Whizzer" White should take a job like that that he would go ahead and get a major in physical education if he stayed in the field very long?

NAISMITH: Well, I don't believe that he would need it. He would be so busy with his football and his basketball and his track that he wouldn't have time to think along in terms of real physical development.

ALLEN: But, Doctor, don't you think he really would get it?

NAISMITH: He ought to have it, certainly. I think that is the trouble. We ought to have lots of things but we can get along without them. But what of the athletics and physical education department? Athletics have a great appeal not only to the instructor but to the public, and also to the principal or superintendent.

ALLEN: Yes, Doctor, but I remember a conversation I had with John Bunn over twelve years ago. He came into my office and said to me, "Doc, I am thinking about changing from what I thought was my life work into another field." John also said, "You know, I have received my degree in engineering. I would like to ask you what is the future in physical education." I said, "John, there is a great future in physical education. If a man will get his M.D. and his Ph.D. degrees, a $20,000 salary in the next twenty years will not be an unheard of thing for the man who prepares for it. John, there will be a lot of small jobs for fellows who partially prepare, but there will only be a few big jobs for men who fit themselves for it." I believe if "Whizzer" White went into coaching he would use that only as an introduction to the plumbing of a deeper life's work. And, Doctor, we do not have to think of "Whizzer" White. There are a great number of other fine athletes who have been brilliant scholars—John Bunn, Junior Coon, Ted O'Leary. And you remember, Doctor, your own football player, Hubert Avery.

NAISMITH: But these men are not in physical education.

ALLEN: That is right, Doctor. Our majors course in physical education was not started in any of our American colleges, in the main, until after the World War. The exception, of course, applies to Columbia, New York University, and Wisconsin. Now there are hundreds and hundreds of colleges in America offering this course. In fact, I do not know of a single college in the state of Kansas, or for that matter, in the land, that does not offer a course in training young men and women in physical education.

NAISMITH: Do you think that most of these colleges that are offering this course are equipped to give a coach a real thorough training in the basic fundamentals for the development of individuals?

ALLEN: Not a fulsome course, Doctor. But there is a demand for this type of work in all the high schools, and many of the graduates from the smaller colleges will accept a position at a salary that gives them employment as a teacher in academic subjects and as a part-time coach. Most of our varsity athletes are engineers, lawyers, journalists, and graduates of the School of Business. It is the business of the University to train professional men, and for that very reason we have not turned out many coaches. However, this newly organized department of physical education, in the School of Education, will supply to the high schools many teachers in physical education and athletic coaching. This has not been true heretofore.

NAISMITH: Now, Doctor, you have touched upon a subject that has been a hobby with me for a number of years. That is that each institution should have a man to look after the physical welfare of the students as head of a department of physical education, employing the instructors in other departments to coach the several teams. Then, when the students or the alumni demand a new coach for the teams this man simply returns to his teaching work, and the department of physical education goes on without interruption.

ALLEN: Perhaps some time the various boards of education of the high schools will accept your splendid theory and obtain both a director of physical education and an athletic coach. Wyandotte High School in Kansas City, Kansas, and in fact, all the high schools in Kansas City, Kansas—Argentino, Rosedale and Wyandotte, have this scheme in operation and it is highly satisfactory. Too many educators and laymen confuse the spectacular phase of athletics with the more prosaic development of the individual. It is very seldom that a coach who is the high-tension, inspirational type of fellow is concerned with the mere serious business of building a department and devotes all his energies to developing the young men under him. When you get a combination of both, the young man you have is ideal. Then if he can organize, deputize and supervise, this set-up is truly a wonderful organization.

NAISMITH: Well, here now, Dr. Allen, you have a basketball game tomorrow night between Oklahoma and the Kansas varsity, opening the Big Six Conference, and you have that old team of ever-victorious Big Six Champions of 1936 coming in to play the superlative performers—the freshmen of this year. Aren't you going to say a word about that?

ALLEN: Well, Dr. Naismith, our time is just about up and we will just let Nelson Sullivan, our sports announcer atop Mount Oread, tell you about this. Thank you very much, Dr. Naismith.

Circular to Public Educators

No Date

A circular directed to public educators about the benefits of basketball as part of a physical education program. No date is associated with this document.

University of Kansas
Lawrence

Division of Physical Education
and
Intercollegiate Athletics

To public educators:

Subject: an obligation to youth.

Forty years ago the physical educators of the country felt the need of a recreative game for adults and Basketball was the result. Today, physical educators are becoming aware of the fact that recreation has invaded the realm of body development and we are going to the extreme of recreative and spectacular games which develop skill and temperament rather than physique and health. By making a fetish of this, we are allowing it to monopolize that time in the life of the school child which is needed for development. I am often asked if basketball is suited to Grade and Junior High Schools. My answer is that it is excellent as a part of the physical education of the child, boy or girl, but as a whole scheme of physical education it is inadequate. It is not, and never was, intended to develop the muscular system, though it will keep the well developed muscular system in good condition.

In an educational system of physical education, part of our duty is to develop the heavier muscular groups, giving a good foundation for the more highly organized nerve controls. In order to accomplish this, it is necessary to give the growing child more or less heavy exercise, which is best obtained by such apparatus as stall bars, adjustable wall ladders, parallel bars, climbing ropes and the various other kinds of apparatus that we find in a well equipped and supervised gymnasium. Most of our games develop the lower extremities while the chest, shoulders and arms are used only to handle some light object. In tumbling and apparatus work, on the other hand, the upper part of the body together with the abdominal muscles are developed. It is in the upper part of the body that the individual lives, the lower extremities being only a means of locomotion. Consequently a large muscular development of the lower extremities and a poor development of the trunk and vital organs is liable to put a strain on the latter.

Basketball should be used as an integral part of Physical Education in the acquiring of skills and reflexes. Basketball has enough interest in itself for all grades of boys and girls so that it is unnecessary to provide artificial stimulus in Grade and Junior High Schools through inter-school contests, or by awarding championships or trophies. This develops a high degree of specialization in skill to the neglect of some other necessary attributes. While basketball is largely a game requiring skill, it demands a good muscular development to maintain the quality of the skills.

The time when this muscular development should be acquired is when nature is stressing this phase of the individual's growth. This comes during the Senior Grades, the Junior High, or even parts of the High School; varying with the individual. This is the period when the pupil should devote most of his time to those exercises that give a symmetrical development of the whole body, stressing those parts which are liable to be neglected in ordinary life. Because he is stressing this phase of his muscular system he need not entirely neglect the development of skills, and some of the higher attributes, nor need he make a fetish of muscular exaggeration as portrayed in some of our magazine advertisements.

3

Rules

After James Naismith created the basic tenants for basketball, he wrote the thirteen rules down on paper and brought them to Mrs. Lyons, the secretary, who typed them and posted them on the wall for the students. There were thirteen original rules and many of them are still the foundation for the game today. For decades, the origins of those "original rules" were unknown even to Naismith as evident in a letter he wrote in 1931. Within a year of the game's invention, Naismith published the first pamphlet discussing the rules. Other than the article in the school's newspaper *The Triangle* that came out in January 1892 introducing this new game, *Rules for Basket Ball* was Naismith's first opportunity to discuss in depth why he developed the game, who it was intended for, and the rules that governed its play. This pamphlet helped spread the game while assisting in its organization in the first few years. By 1894 Naismith wrote three articles for *The Triangle*: "How to Start Basket Ball" (January 1894), "The Umpire in Basket Ball" (March 1894), and "The Referee in Basket Ball" (April 1894). These were his most extensive writings on the game in its infancy. The "Umpire" and "Referee" were later republished by Spalding in 1896–97. As Naismith became involved in other matters over the ensuing decades, he paid less attention to proposed changes to the game. One of the game's early rules was a center jump after each basket. That was eventually eliminated in the mid-1930s. A letter and interview with Dr. Phog Allen, dean of coaching and head basketball coach at the University of Kansas, shed light on his views on that subject.

Original Rules for Basket Ball

December 1891

The original thirteen rules for the game of basketball from December 1891.

BASKET. BALL.

The ball to be an ordinary *Association* foot ball.

1. The ball may be thrown in any direction with one or both hands.
2. The ball may be batted in any direction with one or both hands (never with the fist).
3. A player cannot run with the ball, the player must throw it from the spot on which he catches it, allowance to be made for a man who catches the ball when running at a good speed.
4. The ball must be held in or between the hands, the arms or body must not be used for holding it.
5. No shouldering, holding, pushing, tripping or striking, in any way the person of an opponent shall be allowed. The first infringement of this rule by any person shall count as a foul, the second shall disqualify him until the next goal is made, or if there was evident intent to injure the person, for the whole of the game, no substitute allowed.
6. A foul is striking at the ball with the fist, violation of rules 3 and 4, and such as described in rule 5.
7. If either side makes three consecutive fouls it shall count a goal for the opponents (consecutive means without the opponents in the meantime making a foul).
8. A goal shall be made when the ball is thrown or batted from the grounds [the following in handwriting: into the basket]

and stays there, providing those defending the goal do not touch or disturb the goal. If the ball rests on the edge and the opponent moves the basket it shall count as a goal.

9. When the ball goes out of bounds it shall be thrown into the field, and played by the person first touching it. In case of a dispute the umpire shall throw it straight into the field. The thrower in is allowed five seconds, if he holds it longer it shall go to the opponent. If any side persists in delaying the game, the umpire shall call a foul on them.

10. The umpire shall be judge of the men, and shall note the fouls, and notify the referee when three consecutive fouls have been made. He shall have power to disqualify men according to Rule 5.

11. The referee shall be judge of the ball and shall decide when the ball is in play, in bounds, and to which side it belongs, and shall keep the time. He shall decide when a goal has been made, and keep account of the goals with any other duties that are usually performed by a referee.

12. The time shall be two fifteen minutes halves, with five minutes rest between.

13. The side making the most goals in that time shall be declared the winners. In case of a draw the game may, by agreements of the captains, be continued until another goal is made.

Basket Ball: Rules for Basket Ball

1892

> The first rule book, written by James Naismith, was published in
> 1892, a year after the game was invented. The book was published
> in Springfield, Massachusetts.

Basket Ball is not a game intended merely for amusement, but is the
attempted solution of a problem which has been pressing on physical educators. Most of the games which are played out of doors are
unsuitable for indoors, and consequently whenever the season closes,
the game, together with all the benefits to be derived therefrom, is
dropped. It is true that some players have been accustomed to keep up
a desultory kind of training but it lacked the all-round development
that is so requisite, and very frequently failed to give that training for
the heart and lungs which is so desirable. A number of gymnasiums
have running tracks, but even then it is more or less uninteresting
to run around a gallery so many times per day.

There were certain definite conditions to be met by the game which
was required, and these had to be complied with before it could be
pronounced satisfactory.

1st. It should be such as could be played on any kind of ground,—in
a gymnasium, a large room, a small lot, a large field, whether these
had uneven or smooth surface, so that no special preparation would
be necessary. This is especially necessary in large cities where in
order to get a good sized field you must go to a considerable distance, thus rendering it inaccessible to many of the members. Basket ball may be played on any grounds and on any kind of surface.
It has been played in a gymnasium 12x20 and can be played on an
ordinary foot ball field.

2d. It should be such as could be played by a large number of men at once. This has been fully met, as the only limit to the number of men that can play is the space at command. If a great number of men wish to play at once, two balls may be used at the same time, and thus the fun is augmented though some of the science may be lost. The men however are required to keep their positions a little more carefully. As many as fifty on a side have been accommodated.

3d. It should exercise a man all-round. Every part of his body should get a share of attention. His legs are used to sustain his body and his arms are exercised in handling an object, which is a normal function. In the bendings and twistings of the trunk and limbs the vital organs receive such exercise as will make them healthy and strong. Thus in a manner it serves the same purpose as the sum total of the apparatus of a gymnasium, while the main development is in strict accord with the idea of unity in man. It should cultivate the different energies of which he is capable. Agility is one of the prime requisites in a game where the ball must be secured before an opponent can reach it, and when obtained he must be baffled in his attempt to take it away. This also gives us grace as the perfection of action. Physical judgment is required and cultivated in handling the ball, receiving it from one of your own side, and eluding an opponent. This requires that a man should keep complete control of himself or his play is more than likely to count for nothing. A wrong pass may give the opponent a decided advantage and an instant's hesitation is sufficient to lose the best opportunity that might be offered. There should also be developed that manly courage which is so essential in every true gentleman.

4th. It should be so attractive that men would desire to play it for its own sake. This is one of the chief points in this game. The thorough abandonment of every thought but that of true sport makes it entirely recreative, while the laughable side of the game may be appreciated by both players and spectators. It is made more attractive by the fact that it is a game into which competition may enter and opposing teams may try their skill, thus giving zest to those who have become proficient in the game.

5th. It should have little or none of the reputed roughness of Rugby or Association foot ball, for this reason, kicking the ball and striking at it with the fist were prohibited. All running with the ball was done away with because when a man runs with the ball we necessarily have tackling to stop him, and it is at this point that the roughness of Rugby is most severely felt. This regulation has been criticised specially by Rugby men, but the above reasons should appeal to every one who is seeking a game that can be played without roughness. A man's whole attention is thus centered on the ball and not on the person of an opponent, and thus opportunity for personal spite is taken away. If some of the rules seem unnecessarily severe it should be remembered that the best time to stop roughness is before it begins. A gymnasium is bounded by walls, so that a push which would result in no harm on the soft turf may send a player against the wall with force enough to injure him. If the rules are strictly enforced at first the men will soon get accustomed to playing ball instead of trying to injure those who are opposed to them only for the time being, and they will soon realize that it is nothing but a friendly game. The very men who wish to play roughly will be the first to condemn the game if roughness is allowed, for it is generally they who get the worst of the roughness in the end.

6th. It should be easy to learn. Lacrosse, which is considered one of the best all-round games, has this objection, that it requires too much practice in order to obtain even the exercise from the game, whereas any one can learn to play basket ball at a single lesson, and at the same time obtain the exercise which an experienced player gets.

These were felt to be the conditions that would determine the usefulness of a game that might be played summer and winter, in any climate, and under varying conditions.

The object of a player should be whenever his own side has possession of the ball to gain an uncovered position so that his own side may pass it to him. On the other hand, his opponent should see that he does not gain this favorable position. It is at this point that head work and the ability to do a certain thing without letting his opponent know what he is about to do, are valuable. Individual play does not count for much, for very often a man has to sacrifice his own *chance* of making a goal that he may be sure of it from the hands of another. In the gymnasium the ball as a rule should not be passed swiftly in a straight line, but should be tossed lightly so that the one who receives it shall lose no time in passing it to another or throwing for a goal. But on the field, where long passes may be made, the straight throw may be used to advantage.

Nine men make a nice team for an ordinary sized gymnasium.

A goal keeper; two guards to assist him; a center; a right and left center; two wings and a home man.

These are arranged in this order from the goal which they are defending. A man does not need to keep strictly to his place, but should be always in his own part of the grounds. It should be the duty of the home man and the two wings to get a favorable position to throw for goal and to assist one another in this matter. These ought to be men who are not afraid to sacrifice their own glory for the good of the team, while, at the same time, they should be cool headed enough to use every opportunity of trying for goal. It is often the unexpected that wins. The center men are placed so that they may assist the forwards or help the guards, as the strain comes on each of these. They should be able to make a good shot for goal and quick enough to stop a good play of an opponent. Their aim should be constantly to feed the ball forward to their own men and keep them in a position to make goals. The duty of the guards is principally to prevent the opponents throwing for goal, by preventing them from getting the ball, and by taking it from them when they are preparing to throw. In this, if anywhere, prevention is better than cure, for when a ball is thrown up so as to alight in the basket there is no goal keeper who can keep it from entering. The goal keeper's duty is to get the ball away from the vicinity of his goal and to stop as many plays as possible, thus he will bat the ball more frequently than is advisable in the case of the other players.

When fun and recreation are desired, as many men as please may play, and they may be distributed according to the captain's own idea, but the best plan seems to be to divide the men into three classes, forwards occupying the third of the ground nearest the opponents' goal; center men occupying the middle third; guards occupying the defensive third of the ground. This is not a hard and fast division, but merely to let the men know for what part of the field they are responsible. The men ought to be taught to fill every position, as it is intended to be an all-round game, and though each position entails plenty of hard work yet each man is better if he be able to take any part.

THE GROUNDS

These are the gymnasium floor cleared of apparatus, though any building of this nature would suit. If there is a gallery or running track around the building the baskets may be hung up on this, one at each end, and the bounds marked out on the floor just beneath this gallery. The apparatus may be stored away behind this line and thus be out of the field of play. If there is no gallery the baskets may be hung on the wall, one at each end. In an open field a couple of posts may be set up with baskets on top, and set at the most convenient distance. Out of doors, with plenty of room, the field may be 150 feet long, the goal lines running through the baskets perpendicular to the length of the field; the side boundaries 100 feet apart, but the ball must be passed into the field when behind the goal lines. A player cannot run after he has picked up the ball, though he may throw it and endeavor to get it again; by this means he may make progress from one part of the field to another, but his opponent always has an opportunity of gaining the ball without tackling him. Again, he may bat it in front of him as he runs, or dribble it with his hand along the ground, but he cannot kick it with his feet, not even to dribble it. At a picnic the baskets may be hung on a couple of trees and the game carried on as usual.

GOALS

The goals are a couple of baskets or boxes about fifteen inches in diameter across the opening and, about fifteen inches deep. If the field of play is large the baskets may be larger, so as to allow of more goals being made. When the field is 150 feet long the baskets may be thirty inches in diameter. These are to be suspended, one at each end of the grounds, about ten feet from the floor. A neat device for a goal has been arranged by the Narragansett Machine Company, by which the ball is held and may be thrown out by pulling a string. It is both lasting and convenient.

The object of the game is to put the ball into your opponents' goal. This may be done by throwing the ball from any part of the grounds, with one or both hands, under the following conditions and rules:—

The ball to be an ordinary *Association* foot ball.

1. The ball may be thrown in any direction with one or both hands.
2. The ball may be batted in any direction with one or both hands (never with the fist).
3. A player cannot run with the ball. The player must throw it from the spot on which he catches it, allowance to be made for a man who catches the ball when running if he tries to stop.
4. The ball must be held by the hands, the arms or body must not be used for holding it.
5. No shouldering, holding, pushing, tripping, or striking in any way the person of an opponent shall be allowed; the first infringement of this rule by any player shall count as a foul, the second shall disqualify him until the next goal is made, or, if there was evident intent to injure the person, for the whole of the game, no substitute allowed.
6. A foul is striking at the ball with the fist, violation of Rules 3, 4, and such as described in Rule 5.
7. If either side makes three consecutive fouls it shall count a goal for the opponents (consecutive means without the opponents in the mean time making a foul).
8. A goal shall be made when the ball is thrown or batted *from the grounds* into the basket and stays there, providing those defending the goal do not touch or disturb the goal. If the ball rests on the edges, and the opponent moves the basket, it shall count as a goal.

9. When the ball goes out of bounds, it shall be thrown into the field of play by the person first touching it. He has a right to hold it unmolested for five seconds. In case of a dispute the umpire shall throw it straight into the field. The thrower-in is allowed five seconds, if he holds it longer it shall go to the opponent. If any side persists in delaying the game the umpire shall call a foul on the side.

10. The umpire shall be judge of the men and shall note the fouls and notify the referee when three consecutive fouls have been made. He shall have power to disqualify men according to Rule 5.

11. The referee shall be judge of the ball and shall decide when the ball is in play, in bounds, to which side it belongs, and shall keep the time. He shall decide when a goal has been made, and keep account of the goals, with any other duties that are usually performed by a referee.

12. The time shall be two fifteen minutes, halves, with five minutes' rest between.

13. The side making the most goals in that time shall be declared the winner. In case of a draw the game may, by agreement of the captains, be continued until another goal is made.

The position of umpire is a very responsible one, and on his ruling depends, to a great degree, the value of the game. If he deliberately overlooks violation of the rules he is responsible for a great deal of unnecessary roughness and consequent ill feeling, but if he is firm and impartial in his decisions he will soon win the respect of all, even those who suffered at the time.

When a goal is made it does not cancel the fouls made, neither does half time.

Any player has a right to get the ball at any time when it is in the field of play, provided only that he handles the *ball* and not the opponent. He may slap or pull the ball out of another's hands at any time while in the field of play.

A player may stand in front of the thrower and obstruct the ball, but he must not violate Rule 5. One aim of the rules has been to eliminate rough play, and for this reason the umpire must interpret them with this aim in view.

Any side which persistently makes fouls is working against its own interests, as three consecutive fouls count a goal for the other side. This seemed the best way of compensating those who play a good clean game, and it has proved of value already, for many a team has had two fouls called on them, but very seldom do they make the third, for a team is then on its good behavior, and thus shows that it is possible to play without making many fouls. Setting the number at three gives plenty of room for those made by accident.

How to Start Basket Ball

The Triangle, *January 1894*

> James Naismith wrote an article entitled "How to Start Basket Ball" in January 1894 for *The Triangle*, the publication of the International YMCA Training School.

It is supposed at the outset that the one who is starting the team has a copy of the rules [see pages 40–42 herein], and it is only to further explain the rules that this present article is attempted.

Before putting the men in their places, explain to them that the ball can only be held in the hands, that they cannot run with the ball, that it cannot be kicked or struck with the fist, and that no tackling or holding is allowed. These are the main points which the men will have to keep in mind while playing. The best men with which to start this game are men who have played base ball rather than men who have played foot ball, because the latter are apt to introduce some rough features into the game, whereas base ball men play a more scientific basket ball game than any others.

Let the physical director place a number of men on the floor in the positions described on [pages 34–35 herein], having two teams, the forwards of one team standing near the backs of the other team. Let him take the ball and throw it up in the center of the field just after calling play. The center men will then in all probability either catch the ball and pass it or bat it; the play is then begun in earnest. The ball is thus passed back and forth. At last it crosses out of bounds, one of the players gets it; the director will then explain the different methods of bringing it in as found in rule No. 11. He will also in this connection explain rule No. 7, where a man is not allowed to pass the ball from the field of play out in order to get a free throw, the idea of this rule being that the proper place in which the ball should be kept is inside of the field, and should pass out only as seldom as possible.

When the play has again commenced, in all probability some one will either run with the ball, shoulder or push another one, or in some way make a foul. He will then explain rule No.12 which gives the various fouls that can be made, and also explain the penalty for making a foul, rule 13. He will then put the ball in play, as in rule No. 1, where it says the ball is to be thrown up in the middle of the field after a fouls has been made.

The play again starts as usual. Very soon one man holds the ball between his hands, another man lays his hands upon it, thus holding the ball so that neither can take it away from the other. The referee will then explain rule No. 8, and put it in play again as therein described.

After the play has progressed for a while, some one may claim that he has a right to throw the ball without its being knocked out of his hands, when the director will refer to rule 20 and explain the difference between knocking the ball out of a man's hands and knocking a man's hands off the ball; in the latter case he interferes with the person and not merely takes the ball from his opponent.

If any one claims that the ball is out of bounds in a certain play, the director shall refer to rule No. 10, where it is distinctly stated that the ball is not out of bounds though the person holding it may be; but it is only out of bounds when the ball itself actually crosses the line. Rule No. 9 is worthy of a little explanation where it reads, "The first infringement of this rule shall count a foul, the second shall disqualify" a player. This does not refer to an accidental pushing or striking, but where the intention of the player is to be rough and to handle his opponent regardless of his welfare, and in such a case the umpire shall disqualify him for further play. Any shouldering, pushing or striking shall count a foul.

During the play one of the players in running to get where the ball is catches it in mid-air, but makes two or three steps after he has caught it. The director shall then refer to rule No. 5, where it is said that allowance is to be made for a man who catches the ball while running if he attempts to stop. As regards the last clause of the same rule, a man is allowed to turn in any direction to escape his opponent provided he does not step away from the place on which he stands; so long as one foot remains in its place he may turn in any direction, but should he turn on one foot placing the other foot in a convenient place and then attempt to turn on the foot which he has already moved, it will count as a foul.

Again, if a player in attempting to take the ball from another should hold it in his arms or press it to his chest, the director will then refer to rule No. 6.

A player attempts to put the ball in the basket and someone jumping up strikes the basket and knocks the ball off. The director shall then refer to the last clause of rule No. 13. If the ball rebounds from the sides of the building or from the gallery, the same rule covers the point when it shall be counted a goal. If anyone who is not playing interferes with the ball in a try for goal, then rule No. 15 shall be referred to.

This covers the chief points which are to be remembered in playing the game. Some directors line up the men at opposite ends of the field and when the ball is thrown up, let them rush for their positions. This is neither scientific nor safe, as in a rush of this kind there is sure to be not only confusion but injury, so that the men always occupy the positions which they are to keep before the ball is put in play. In appointing a referee and umpire, it is absolutely essential that they should understand the game and that they should be ready to do their duty without respect to persons or without delay.

The Umpire in Basket Ball

The Triangle, *March 1894*

> James Naismith wrote an article titled "The Umpire in Basket Ball"
> in March 1894 for *The Triangle*, the publication of the International
> YMCA Training School.

As seen in rule 19, the umpire shall be judge of the men. His first
duty will be to get well in mind the rules which govern the action of
the men on the field; as for instance, rules 4, 5, 6, 9, 16 and 19. In all
his decisions he must note that the spirit of the game is that *there
shall be no rough play*, and that *his duties are to see that no rough
play occurs*. He will remember that the rules as found in the book
are merely to guide him in this matter rather than a letter which cannot be broken, and if an occasion arises where a man is manifestly
rough, even though he should not violate the letter of any rule, and
should attempt to claim exemption from a foul, it is the umpire's
duty to rule according to the circumstances. He will find authority
for this in rule 19.

In order to be a successful umpire, a man must confine his attention entirely to the men during the time of play. There is a tendency
on the part of the umpires to follow the ball, rather than to follow the
movements of the men themselves. Thus, he requires a good deal of
judgment, and should endeavor to locate where the ball is going to
alight whenever it is thrown in the air, or should endeavor to locate
the men who are about to receive the ball rather than to follow its
flight. If an umpire will constantly keep this in mind, he will be able
to detect fouls more quickly than if he does not thus concentrate his
attention. It is absolutely essential that the umpire should pay the
strictest attention to his business, and it is only by doing this that he
will ever be able to watch from ten to eighteen men.

An umpire should give full scope for team play, and remember that a man is entitled to his position on the floor, and it is the man who pushes another out of the way upon whom the foul should be called. Thus, if a man stands still, with his arms extended, and another player rushes against his arms, you cannot call a foul on the former because he has made no motion whatever, and were a man thus compelled to give way for an opponent, the play, of course, could not be carried on; but if this same man should show by his actions that he was endeavoring to get his arm around the other so as to hold him and keep him from getting away, it would be the umpire's duty then to call a foul on him. In this case, as in a great many others, an umpire must use his own judgment.

As for the rules themselves: No. 4 is easily ruled upon. The object of this is to prevent injury, and if a man strikes with his fists, he may very readily use that as an excuse for striking his opponent. The ball must not be kicked. That does not mean that a man may not place his foot so as to stop the ball.

In No. 5, a player cannot run with the ball. This is to prevent roughness, because wherever a man is allowed to run with the ball, the opposing side must be given the privilege of stopping him. It was, for this reason, that all running was prohibited. So long as one foot remains on the spot where the ball was caught and the other swung round, it is not considered running.

The ball must not be so held that an opponent has not a fair opportunity of taking it away; this is the spirit of rule No. 6. Thus, it cannot be held by the arms, legs or body; it must be handled entirely by the hands.

Rule No. 9 is inserted for the purpose of preventing rough play, and any roughness which does not come under the head of shouldering, holding, pushing, tripping or striking, is not, therefore, necessarily to be permitted, as rule No. 19 will show. The second clause of No. 9 is not for the purpose or ruling off a man who, as it were, almost by accident, holds, pushes, etc., but one who is intentionally rough and regardless of others. A man is supposed to be a gentleman, and the moment that he shows himself to be other than this, then it becomes the umpire's duty to protect the other players. In order to aid the umpire in determining when a man is holding, it is well to consider that when a man has both arms around another, he is guilty of holding; for if a man has both arms around another, the umpire cannot tell whether he is holding or not, and for this reason it is well to rule according to this idea. This rule holds good outside of bounds as well as in.

Rule No. 16 is to prevent a team which is manifestly outplayed, from delaying the game in order that the score may not be great.

Rule No. 20 is one which the umpire needs to watch carefully, because very frequently in the attempt which one man makes to get the ball from his opponent, he may strike the other player; yet he has full liberty to knock the ball out of the other man's hands.

It is often difficult to decide, when a man is dribbling the ball, whether he carries it or not. It is not permissible to dribble at all with the feet, but it is perfectly permissible to roll the ball along the ground, which might be called dribbling, so long as the hands leave the ball while it is on the ground; but merely shoving the ball along the ground will rank as a foul, because in that case, the opponent is not given an opportunity of getting the ball.

Again, jumping with the ball in the hands and touching the ground at each jump is carrying the ball. Again, throwing the ball up on the palm of the hand is carrying it; but if the ball be thrown higher than the head, it would not be considered carrying. A man has no right to fall on the ball in the field of play; he would then render himself liable to have a foul called for holding the ball with the body, but a man accidentally falling on the ball would not thus be liable. Again, holding the ball against another man's body in order to have a foul called on him, is not permissible; it should then be counted a foul so the person so holding, because he is really holding the man when he holds the ball against him. The spirit of the game is fair play, and this violates all the spirit of gentlemanly playing.

In league games between different associations, it is well to have the same man umpire all the games, if possible, as it is the fairest way of doing. It is needless to say that this man should have no interest in any of the teams of the league; especially should he not be the physical director, or anyone else coaching the team, because a man in that position will either be too strict on his own team or be blamed by the opponents for not ruling strictly enough; but in cases where it is impossible to get a man who understands the game, it might be better to permit the coach to umpire.

The Referee in Basket Ball

The Triangle, *April 1894*

James Naismith write an article entitled "The Referee in Basket Ball" in April 1894 for *The Triangle*, the publication of the International YMCA Training School.

The referee has full control of the game, therefore, his first duty is to see that all necessary arrangements have been made before the game commences, so that as little trouble as possible shall arise afterwards, and that his decisions may be fairly given. He should see that the peculiarities of the gymnasium are explained to the captains of the teams, and when any special rules are necessary, they should be clearly defined to both captains before the game commences. He should also see that the goals have been properly protected from the spectators, see rule No. 15. He shall toss with the captains for choice of goal, and change goals at half-time. He shall put the ball in play, as in rule No. 1.

The main part of his duties is defined in rule No. 18, where it says that he shall be judge of the ball; for this reason it is necessary that he keep his eyes constantly on the ball instead of the men, as in the case of the umpire. He must decide whether or not it crosses the boundary line, see rule No. 10, and when it does cross, to whom the ball belongs. Rule No. 11 says that it shall be returned by the side first holding it. This does not mean that there may be a scrimmage for the ball, nor yet does it necessarily imply that it belongs to the first man touching it, but whenever it is clear to the mind of the referee that one side or the other has possession of it, he shall award it to that side.

Whenever he is in doubt as to which of the players has the ball, he shall, as in Rule 11, throw it up in the field himself, not necessarily carrying it to the center of the field, but throwing it in from the spot where he picks it up. He also shall watch the ball that he may tell when it drops into the basket. He shall also note the spot from which it is thrown, as a goal cannot be thrown from out of bounds. Especially shall he be careful where the goals that are used are without bottoms, for sometimes it is hard to distinguish when it really passes through. It is much better, both for the referee and the spectators, that the baskets should have bottoms, as it helps him in his decisions, and is more attractive to the spectators, who enjoy seeing the ball deposited in the basket. He must also note when the ball rests on the top of the basket, especially if the opponents should move the goal, as found in rule No. 13.

Whenever the ball has been thrown out of the field of play, so that none of the players can get it, it shall go to the referee before again being put in play. The referee also decides rule No. 7, when the ball merely changes hands. Rule No. 8 also comes under his jurisdiction. This is to prevent any roughness, when several men are trying to get possession of the ball; but if one side is evidently doing this to kill time, he shall then call the attention of the umpire to rule No. 16. He shall not interfere with any decision of the umpire, as the latter is authority in his own sphere.

Whenever it is necessary to call time, the referee shall blow his whistle, and no play can be made after the whistle is blown; but if the ball has left the player's hands when the whistle blows, and it alights in the basket, it shall then count a goal. The referee and umpire shall each carry a whistle, and whenever this is blown, the play shall cease, until the referee again puts the ball in play, as in Rule 1. The referee shall also keep an accurate account of the fouls and goals made, and score according to rule No. 14. He shall also decide at the close to whom the game belongs, and how the score stands.

Any points which do not fall within the jurisdiction of the umpire belongs to the referee.

This series of articles, by Mr. Naismith, will be put in book form, and published by The Triangle Publishing Co., with Rules for 1894.

Letter to Robert H. Sturm

January 7, 1930

A letter written by James Naismith to Robert H. Sturm on January 7, 1930, in which he gives his thoughts on the center jump. Printed on KU letterhead, it was unsigned and may not be complete.

University of Kansas
Lawrence, Kansas

Office of
James Naismith, M. D.
Inventor of Game of Basketball
Honorary Life Member of Rules Committee
Honorary Chairman of Rules Committee
Honorary President Basketball Coaches Association

1./ 7./ 30.

Mr. R. H. Sturm
Indianapolis Ind.

My dear Sir:-
    Last night I watched with great care and much interest an illustration of two substitutes for the center tip off. One where the ball was put in play from behind the opponents goal line, the other where it was put in play from a point ten feet behind the centre of the field. Each of these resulted in the same style of play viz. an attack on the five man defense. This made the game monotonous to the spectators and limited the possibilities of the players. Many plays have been devised around the center play some of those when the opponents control the tip off and some

where the team has the advantage and others where neither can consistently control the play.

One coach in his book on basketball has seventeen plays at the center and seven in other positions. Another has twenty at the center and nine in other positions. In the substitutes tried last night all these would be useless and the plays limited to those attacking the five man defense.

All games with two goals start from the centre of the field and in those games where the men are scattered the opening play is between two players e.g. Hockey, lacrosse, field hockey, and polo.

In the early nineties football could be put in play from scrimmage and the opening play was just like the rest of the plays. This was changed and the kick off is compulsory.

The objection to the tip off is that it gives an advantage to the tall center. There are several ways in which the center play can be retrained and this factor eliminated. First by limiting the height of the man who takes the tip off, thus retaining all the spectacular elements and retaining the plays around center. Or the tip off may be rotated between the persons who are natural opponents. This is done in volley ball. Or a still further element of chance might be introduced by permitting the opposing captain to select the center. However the simplest method is for the referee to toss the ball up high in the air and make the centers wait to judge their time to jump, thus adding another element to the requisites for a good center. At present the players jump with the motion of the referee and as it rises just above the tall men's fingers he has a decided advantage.

Investigations have been made as to the value of the control at center and it has been found that almost 50% of the controlled tips go to the other team. In a recent game when one center was four inches taller than the other the tall man controlled the tip out of 27 times ten times the shorter player seven and uncontrolled 10 times. In the same game there was one goal made where the ball did not pass to the opponents.

Letter to Dr. J. H. McCurdy

June 6, 1931

Letter written by James Naismith to Dr. J. H. McCurdy on June 6, 1931, in which he discusses the present location of the original rules of basketball.

University of Kansas
Lawrence

Division of Physical Education and Intercollegiate Athletics

June 6, 1931

Dr. J. H. McCurdy,
Springfield College Alumni Association,
Springfield, Massachusetts.

My dear McCurdy:

Unfortunately I can not put my hands upon the original set of rules which have put away as they are fading and I want to preserve them as long as possible. I have, however, a photograph of these original rules and if you would think these satisfactory, I will send them to you.

My later photograph is about 6 x 8 but I have one that was taken a couple years ago which is 8 x 10. I will send whichever of these you wish.

I have not had time to think up the idea of the exhibition as we are in the midst of our examinations which I have just concluded and I shall now be able to give some time to it.

I am sorry that it will be impossible for me to get to Springfield for the commencement as this is our anniversary.

With kind personal regards, I am

Most sincerely yours,
James Naismith.
Prof. Phys. Education.

The Tip-less Game of Basketball

Radio Program, January 13, 1938

A radio interview between Dr. Forrest "Phog" Allen and James
Naismith on January 13, 1938, entitled "The Tip-less Game of
Basketball."

ALLEN: Dr. Naismith, I would like to ask you a question. After 45
years of starting your game of basketball with the center tip, the
rules committee last April eliminated the tip after field and foul
goals. In your opinion, why did they do this?

NAISMITH: Well, in originating the game, after considerable
thought as to how the ball would be put in play, the center tip
seemed the only reasonable way of giving each side an equal
chance of obtaining the ball. Now, the only objection that I can
see to it is that the tall player monopolizes the tip-off because of
his heights and the assistance of the referee who tosses it up in
such a manner that the tall man has a better chance of obtaining it than the short man. There are several ways in which this
might have been corrected. Now that is my idea. Doctor, what is
yours? You are on the Rules Committee, and attended the meeting in which the National Rules body voted it out. Why did they
do this?

ALLEN: Well, Dr. Naismith, I find myself agreeing with you on the
center tip-off. I have always believed in it. I have always contended that in football we have the kick off at the start of the
game. I feel that the tip-off at the start of the game of basketball, and after each goal, is just as vital because it tends to give
both sides an equal advantage. At the Rules meeting I found
myself in a very great minority, and as is the habit with all of
these committee gatherings, the minority goes along peace-

ably with the majority. I felt that if the majority desired it, it was only fair to give them a chance without protesting violently against it. I still think basketball has enough thrills for the spectators and the players in the tipless game. I found many of the rules-makers blaming all the ills of basketball on the tall man at the tip-off. Really, I think that because the basket is only 10 feet from the floor that we are blaming a man for being too tall under a 10-foot basket, because those tall players can actually dunk the ball into the basket. Some of the tall players can actually reach 8 inches above the basket. In my opinion, the goal should be out of reach of all players.

NAISMITH: Well, the things you have said are still not a sufficient reason to me to do away with a fair and spectacular method and substitute one that is less so.

ALLEN: Dr. Naismith, I still agree with you 100 per cent, because it is the tall man that beats you under the defensive or offensive basket by reaching higher than his teammates in obtaining the ball. No player may pull his opponents' arms down when he has the ball in his possession, because that is holding. But, Doctor, they blame that tall fellow tapping the ball in the center of the court for all the ills of the past game. I have heard one of our own boys, Coach Arthur "Dutch" Lonborg, of Northwestern University say many times that he found when his team had a short center and could not control the tip-off that in those very years he had his scrappiest teams. Those boys with their apparent disadvantage had to fight harder than ever to recover the ball after the tip-off.

NAISMITH: Well, Doctor, that is a good point. Now, another question—is there any other game in which there is not either an equal chance for the opponents to obtain the ball after a goal is made, or the defendants are compelled to drive the ball into the opponents' territory? In the early '90s in football the ball was given to one side at the beginning of the game and after the goal was made, they were permitted to attack instead of the usual kick off. This lasted about two years, and then the return to the kick off was made.

ALLEN: Dr. Naismith, do you think that the game of basketball as now constituted has a similar opportunity?

NAISMITH: I am not sure as to that. If the game is better without the tip-off certainly it will not return. Only time will tell about that. We want the game to continuously make progress.

ALLEN: Doctor, one critic in Indianapolis contended that you are still in the era of the peach-basket stage. What would be your reaction to such criticism as that?

NAISMITH: If I am in the peach-basket stage it is because the late rules compel me to be in that stage. In the early days 10 men played the game in a 40 by 50 foot area, and we gradually enlarged the field so as to get in scientific plays. But the rules since 1932 are now compelling 10 men to play in a space 45 by 50 feet which naturally brings in a lot of roughness as we had in the peach basket stage, and the center tip is the only play that occupies the full court.

ALLEN: Well, Dr. Naismith, this is a tribute to you when they talk about the peach basket stage, because the basket idea was yours, and I would say that any idea that can enthrall 18 million people is a peach of an idea! But, seriously, Doctor, the proponents of the new rule state that this new rule has increased the playing time about 7 minutes. What do you say as to that?

NAISMITH: Do you think that is right? In the rule it specifically states that the ball is dead after a goal is made and play ceases, and how can you increase the playing time? You might decrease the elapsed time, but you can't increase the playing time.

ALLEN: That is exactly right, Doctor. They have not increased the playing time one iota by rule. But they can actually play longer under this game than they played under last year's game. This is the reason: After a free throw or a field goal was made the referee tossed the ball up at center for the tip-off. By research it was determined that it took on an average about 10 seconds for the ball to be brought from the end line where the basket was made to the center at the time it was tossed up for the tip-off, and incidentally that 10 seconds gave the spectators time to catch their breath and their hearts to resume normalcy after a thrilling score. Counting the number of field goals and free throws that were successfully made, and multiplying this by 10 seconds, the total elapsed time during the progress of the game was 5 to 7 minutes. Had the time been declared out last year after field goals, the playing situation would have been identically the same as this year.

NAISMITH: Well, now, according to the wording of the new rule, how can the game be speeded up on account of the rules? Is it not in spite of the rules that the game has been speeded up?

ALLEN: Well, Doctor, so far as the speeding up of the game is concerned, that is entirely up to the play of the two opposing teams. The so-called new rules have not been in the books long enough for the teams to get thoroughly adjusted, as yet. If the side scored upon really desires to delay the game, that side may hold the ball 5 seconds out of bounds by rule at the end line before they throw the ball in, and then they may take 10 seconds in addition before the players on that side are forced by the rule to cross the center line of the court, or the division line. In other words, it is possible to withhold the ball from the offensive court for 14 seconds after a goal is made. So you can see that they can play the slow break just as well as they can play the fast break, and personally I think that some smart team is going to try that. I noticed by Sunday's paper that Iowa State used the slow break against Kansas State and beat them 41 to 30. So you see, Doctor, all teams are not going in for this fire department basketball. In another year I predict that many teams will be using the slow break and then you will have 5 seconds to pass the ball in from out of bounds and 10 seconds to get across. Then after they get across they are going to use a play that many people call "stall", and it will be a dreary game. Don't you think so?

NAISMITH: Yes, I certainly agree with you. That is the real objection to the whole thing, and that has been and is my objection to the tipless center. It gives the team that has been scored upon an opportunity to delay the game.

ALLEN: Well, then, Doctor, who knows but what your prophecy, although you didn't prophesy you did indicate, that since the football rules went back to the kick off there may be a return to the center tip-off in basketball in a year or two. Don't you think there is a possibility of rotating the jumpers in basketball just as they have the batting order in baseball? The coaches could instruct their players during practice, so it would be an easy matter to handle the game situation.

NAISMITH: And another thing, Dr. Allen—if there was a deviation from this practice by any one team, the opponent would quickly recognize it and call it to the attention of the referee.

ALLEN: Why, certainly they would. No difficulty would be encountered in this regard. But, Doctor, I see that our time is fast drawing to a close.

NAISMITH: But wait a minute—at least we have time for another question, haven't we?

ALLEN: Surely.

NAISMITH: A great deal has been said about the injurious effects of the fast break, especially in league games among junior high schools. Don't you think that they are putting too much stress upon the contest rather than upon the recreative sport and educational factors for the young boys?

ALLEN: Yes, Doctor. Instances of this have come up often in the National Rules discussion. I remember distinctly that Floyd Rowe, director of physical education of the public schools of Cleveland, Ohio, submitted a research finding that was done in Cleveland. This research showed that organized league competition actually affected the nervous system of these boys to such an extent that the normal growth was influenced. One group was taken with no special emphasis upon league play and the other group indulged in regular league competition. According to the findings in Cleveland, the regular league competition was very detrimental to high school boys under the old rule, and under the new rule the strenuosity of the game would be increased. I am sure that the authorities who are making surveys would certainly be against this new game on that principle.

NAISMITH: Well, now, isn't this league contest a strain upon the nervous system rather than upon the muscular? And for my part, I think that it would be very much better to limit the league playing or the interscholastic competition in the junior high schools.

ALLEN: Yes, Doctor, you have hit the nail right on the head, because isn't it true that the nervous system controls the glandular system, and the glandular system determines the growth of the individual?

NAISMITH: That is my idea of it.

ALLEN: By the way, we have Nelson Sullivan, our sports announcer atop Mr. Oread. Sully, you tell the wide world the news, will you?

4

Basketball in Canada

A Canadian by birth, James Naismith invented the game while a professor at the International YMCA Training School in Springfield, Massachusetts. His first class contained several fellow Canadians who, after graduating, returned to Canada where they played important roles in introducing the game to their country. Nearly forty years after he invented the game, Naismith inquired about the game's history in Canada as well as some of the Canadian students in his class. The series of letters that follow highlight the roles some of those individuals played in introducing the game to Canada. Since those early days, basketball has had a rich history in Canada as evidenced today by the numbers of Canadians excelling in the National Basketball Association (NBA). One of the earliest teams that garnered international success was the Edmonton Grads, a women's professional barnstorming team. In his tribute, Naismith proudly recognizes the achievements and success of this team on and off the court.

Letters on Basketball in Canada

1930

A series of letters written in 1930 between James Naismith, J. H. Crocker, and T. D. Patton concerning the history of basketball in Canada.

December 15, 1930

Mr. J. H. Crocker,
Acting Secretary,
Department of Physical Education,
Young Men's Christian Association.
40 College Street,
Toronto, Canada.

My dear Mr. Crocker:

Many thanks for the interest you have in the game of basket ball and for the information that you have given to me.

I wonder if you could give me any information as to the present location of any of the members of the first basket ball team. Especially those who went into Canada; Mr. Lyman Archibald, Mr. A. B. Chase, Mr. Thompson, myself and maybe one other in that group of Canadians. Also I should like very much to have their addresses and occupations of as many of those men as you know. Some of them may still be in the Y. M. C. A. work in Canada.

In looking over the catalogue of the Springfield Y. M. C. A. College I failed to find any mention of any member of that team, so I do not know whether they are still alive or whether they have simply gone out of the work. I know that Mr. Mann who was captain of the team is dead. I had a communication not

long ago from his son who is in physical education work somewhere in New England.

Any information that you can give me along this line, or in
connection with basket ball; especially as to the extent of the
number of persons playing the game, whether in the Y. M. C. A.
or in Canada in general will be greatly appreciated.

With kindest personal regards I am

Most sincerely yours,
James Naismith.
Professor Physical Education

The National Council of Young Men's
Christian Associations of Canada
40 College Street, Toronto-2

December 11, 1930.

Dr. Jas. Naismith,
University of Kansas,
Lawrence, Kansas.

Dear Dr. Naismith:

I was glad to have your letter of December 4th and I regret
very much that I can not give you much more detail about basketball in Canada than was contained in my letter of February
10th, 1928; but as I remember the early days it was as follows:

Lyman Archibald, who had graduated from Springfield, came
to St. Stephen, New Brunswick, in the fall of 1892 and one of
the first games that he introduced was basketball. We were
then playing nine men a side, and during that first winter we
had games between the different sections of the Association
membership.

Later on in the year the game was introduced to Milltown,
N.B., and Calais, Maine, both places nearby, and we played some
games together.

In 1894 I became General Secretary of the Amherst Association and introduced the game there, which seems to be the first which they had in Nova Scotia.

After leaving St. Stephen, Lyman Archibald came to Hamilton, Ontario, where there was a much larger membership. Here he introduced the game in 1893 and it made rapid progress, and Hamilton has always continued to be a great basketball centre.

I am sending a copy of this letter to Mr. T.D. Patton, asking him to give you particulars of the game in Montreal and Ottawa, as well as in Winnipeg.

Through the courtesy of "T.D." I have in my possession a copy of the first rules and a picture of the first group. If either of these would be of value to you for reference, I would be very glad indeed to loan them to you. They are now part of our historical collection in this office.

I hope you are going to be able to succeed in giving us a good history of the early days of basketball as you are the only one who can give a continuous picture of the game which has spread more rapidly than any other in the history of physical education.

With kind regards, I beg to remain

Faithfully yours,
J. H. Crocker
Acting Secretary,
Department of Physical Education.

December 11, 1930.

Mr. T.D. Patton,
19 Nanton Ave.,
Toronto.

Dear T.D.:
I enclose herewith copy of letter which I have just written to Dr. Naismith, which will more or less explain itself.

If Dr. Naismith has not written you I wish you would write and give him details as you remember them regarding Ball starting the game of basketball in Montreal and your early experience with the development of the game in Winnipeg.

I hope that the genial Doctor may be able to get us a good history of basketball before he finishes his activities in the realm of physical education, otherwise much of that history will never be written.

Faithfully yours,
JHC
Acting Secretary,
Department of Physical Education.

February 10th, 1930.

Dr. James Naismith,
University of Kansas,
Lawrence, Kansas,
U.S.A.

Dear Dr. Naismith:

I have been in touch with T. D. Patton recently, and he has been insistent that I write you with reference to the basketball development in New Brunswick.

In conversation with Mr. W.H. Ball, a short time ago, he informed me that basketball was started in Montreal during the winter of '91 and '92.

I know that basketball was started in St. Stephen, N.B., by Lyman Archibald who graduated from Springfield in 1891, going to St. Stephen in the fall of '92. During that winter we organized basketball and continued with the game, and it spread all through the Maritime Provinces.

I have before me a copy of the rules for basketball issued by yourself in 1892. Mr. T.D. Patton has given us a copy of the photo of the original group, a reproduction of which we forwarded to the Sports Publishing Company, who published the same in the basketball rule book of this year. If there are any further details with which I can assist you, I would be very glad, indeed, to do so if you will let me know what you require.

Faithfully yours,
JIIC
Secretary,
Physical Education Department.

Dr. Naismith's Tribute to the "Grads"

No Date

Tribute written by James Naismith regarding the Edmonton Grads
women's basketball team. No date associated with this tribute.

No other name in basketball is revered to the same extent as that
of the late Dr. James A. Naismith, the inventor of the game, and a
former member of the faculty of the University of Kansas. The following tribute which Dr. Naismith so kindly paid to the "Grads" is,
therefore, all the more striking:

To the Commercial Grads, Past and Present:
Permit me to add my hearty congratulations to the many that
must have poured in from your host of friends and admirers
on this your twenty-first birthday. Your record is without parallel in the history of basketball. There is no team that I mention more frequently in talking about the game. My admiration
is not only for your remarkable record of games won (which of
itself would make you stand out in the history of basketball) but
also for your record of clean play, versatility in meeting teams at
their own style, and more especially for your unbroken record
of good sportsmanship. It is the combination of all these things
that makes your record so wonderful.

My admiration and respect go to you also because you have
remained unspoiled by your success, and have retained the
womanly graces notwithstanding your participation in a strenuous game. You are not only an inspiration to basketball players throughout the world, but a model for all girls' teams. Your
attitude and success have been a source of gratification to me in

illustrating the possibilities of the game in the development of the highest type of womanhood.

This message would not be complete without a reference to my good friend Mr. Percy Page, who, of course, is chiefly responsible for your success. You are indeed fortunate in having a man like Mr. Page as your coach, for I regard him as the greatest coach and the most superb sportsman it has ever been my good fortune to meet.

Most sincerely yours,
(Sig.) James Naismith.

5

Correspondence

Today trash talking an opponent on the playground, in the back-
yard, or on a basketball court is part of the culture of basketball. It
is a form of trying to get an advantage over or in the head of your
opponent. The earliest form of trash talking might have occurred
in 1894, a few years after the game was invented. A series of teams
of students and faculty at the International YMCA Training School
was formed with the goal of claiming the gym championship. These
teams had nicknames such as Lions, Snakes, Tree-tops, and Lambs,
over which Naismith presided. The letters included within show
the fun that each of these teams had as they competed for the gym
title. Some of the letters contain poems, some a warning. In each
instance, the passion and desire to compete and defeat their colleagues comes through clearly as basketball had an ability to unite
people, even in the game's early years.

Formal Challenges

January 11, 1894

A series of correspondence—letters and poems—written by team managers of student and faculty teams at the International YMCA Training School in January 1894.

Springfield, Mass., Jan. 11, 1894.
Room 56 Winchester Park Building.

Greeting:

Know all men by these presents that I, Albert B. Chase, manager of the Jungle Basket Ball Team, by virtue of my authority, do hereby on this eleventh day of January in the year of our Lord one thousand eight hundred and ninety four set forth this greeting to the occupants of the Winchester Park Building, and all Basket Ball teams contained therein.

Whereas the cause of basket ball in the Winchester Park Building is in rather a dormant condition, and

Whereas some remarks detrimental to the excellent reputation of the inhabitants of the Jungle as basket ball players have been circulated,

Be it resolved therefore, by the inhabitants of the Jungle, that as the honor of the aforementioned place is at stake, we jointly and severally make known our determination to acquit ourselves of all such injurious remarks.

Therefore, be it known that the Jungle Basket Ball Team is ready to meet any team composed of members of any one alley in the Winchester Park Building to compete for the supremacy of the aforesaid place, Maiden Lane or Faculty Row preferred.

For arrangement of games apply to Albert B. Chase, Manager Jungle Basket Ball Team, Room 56, Jungle, or E. P. Ruggles, Room 53.

Given under my hand on this eleventh day of January in the year of our Lord one thousand eight hundred and ninety four.

> E P Ruggles, Capt.
> Albert B. Chase,
> M'g'r.

"Long may the forest tops wave in the Jungle,
　　Long may the lion roar in his lair,
Long may the snakes tie themselves in a bundle
　　And may all games be played on the square."

. . .

WHEREAS, The game of Basket Ball is being very extensively
　　played (on paper); and
WHEREAS, Many challenges and no games constitute the present record; therefore,
BE IT RESOLVED, That the Midway Plaisance Basket Ball team
　　believes in Basket Ball rather than in vocal bawling; and
BE IT RESOLVED, That the above mentioned team is ready to
　　compete in the specified game on the *floor* rather than on
　　paper; and,
BE IT FURTHER RESOLVED, That we hereby accept each and
　　every challenge now before the School.

"By their fruits ye shall know them."
"Actions speak louder than words."

I have read in a fresh but marvelous tale,
　　In a legend strangely queer,
That a wonderous host of challenges
　　In the Training School Hall Appear.

White as a snowbank specked with fleas,
    The bluffing host is seen.
And wonder's stamped on every face
    As the students file between.

Down in the gym, quick and sure,
    The decision will be made,
On the highest shelf that host
    Of bluffers shall be laid.

    W. V. Dinsan.
    Manager.

• • •

To all whom it may concern:-

Inasmuch as some have taken in hand to set forth an orderly—likewise poetical—declaration of the merits of their respective Basket Ball teams, it has seemed good to some others also, who have had some understanding of this noble and exhilarating game, to effect a combination for the purpose of testing the understanding, as also the skill, of the Denizens of the Jungle, Habitues of the Midway Plaisance, Toughs of the Bowery, Emigrants of Castle Garden, and the friskiness of "The Lambs" of Faculty Row.

Be it know, therefore, that the "Hard Shells" do herby challenge the respective teams of the above mentioned localities, or of any other locality, to engage for supremacy in Basket Ball, whether it be gamboling with "The Lambs," conflict sanguinary with the jungleites, exhibiting feats of skill of surpassing interest, even to the fakirs of the Plaisance, or a "go" with bare knuckles with the Boweryites, etc., etc.

Challenges heretofore published have been framed with sufficient diplomacy to exclude the possibility of meeting the team representing outside interest—doubtless for fear of disastrous results to themselves. In consideration of this fact, therefore, the challenge is extended to all comers, of whatever name, nationality, or color; height or shortness; degree of emaciation or girth of waist; length of limb or bigness of head.

What, [ ] Ye brave men who think that to breathe[1]
   The air in your classical hall,
Is all that's required to fully prepare
   A team that can play Basket Ball;

And Ye who accustomed to sit in your chairs,
   And wither us all with a look,
And think that our power may be shown in the hour
   We recite, while you look in a book;

And ALL who desire the game thus to use,
   In winning themselves a fair name,
Feel honored! We claim you as the stepping-stones broad,
   To lift us to Honor and Fame.

By this act of our hand, we think we can prove,
   In about the small space of a minute,
That, tho' we don't live 'neath this sheltering roof,
   We are yet most emphatically "in it."

   • • •

Behold the Faculty,
Ready to tackle ye,
And though ye may jibe and cry,
What's a name?
When repeated we call,
In your baskets the ball,
'Tis plain you will have naught to reply,
But——they're game!

To our friends, the denizens of The Jungle: Lions, Snakes, Tree-tops, and all others, GREETING:

Realizing the importance of the matters referred to in your manifesto of Jan. 11th, after due deliberation, we have decided to offer ourselves to the glory-hungry appetites of you, our friends. We trust that the final arrangements may be rapidly made for the consummation of the much-to-be-desired game. There is but one lion amongst us, and she, sad to relate, is a young, meek, mild-mannered, woman. Sometimes, however, in times of great excitement, such have been known to equal the strongest and bravest. In our great desire to take no undue advantage of you, our friends, the enemy, we hereby agree not to engage her in the conflict. Thus, we shall be in fact, as well as in name, "THE LAMBS."

We are ready to do our part in hastening the time when the inhabitants of The Jungle and the lambs may lie down together. If the fates ordain that the lambs shall be inside, we shall not attempt to alter their firm decree, but shall toughen ourselves so that although swallowed, we shall not be severed.

Soon will the forest-tops droop in The Jungle,
Soon will the lion howl in despair,
Soon will the snakes begin to unbundle,
Provided the game is played on the square.

Jas. Naismith
Mgr

Notes on Sources

The author wishes to thank several individuals and repositories for their assistance in locating and granting permission to publish these documents. Every effort has been made to properly acknowledge each source.

McGill University
Letter to Mr. Morgan, August 14, 1928

 McGill University Archives, *McGill News*, Fall 1992

Springfield College
Advertisement in *The Triangle*, January 1892
Basket Ball, 1894
"Basket Ball," *The Triangle*, January 1892
"Basketball—a Game the World Plays," *The Rotarian*,
 January 1939
Basket Ball: Rules for Basket Ball, 1892
Duck on a rock rules, no date
Formal challenges, January 11, 1894
Fundamentals of Basketball, 1910
"History of Basketball," *Young Men's Era*, April 16, 1896
"How Basketball Started and Why It Grew So Fast," 1931
"How to Start Basket Ball," *The Triangle*, January 1894
Letter to Dr. J. H. McCurdy, June 6, 1931
Letter to Mr. R. G. Roberts, January 23, 1937
Letter to Thomas Browne, April 7, 1898
Memorandum of conference, March 23, 1939
"The Origin of Basket Ball," January 5, 1932
"The Referee in Basket Ball," *The Triangle*, April 1894
Thomas Browne letter, August 4, 1943
"The Umpire in Basket Ball," *The Triangle*, March 1894

Courtesy of Springfield College, Babson Library, Archives and Special Collections

University of Kansas

"Basketball's Place in the Physical Education Program," radio program, January 6, 1938

"The Tip-less Game of Basketball," radio program, January 13, 1938

Kenneth Spencer Research Library, University of Kansas Libraries

"Basket Ball," presented at the Eight Annual Conference of the National Collegiate Athletic Association, reprinted in the *American Physical Education Review*, May 1914

"Dr. Naismith's Tribute to the 'Grads,'" no date

Original rules for basket ball, December 1891

Radio interview, December 15, 1932

We the People, radio program, January 31, 1939, https://exhibits.lib.ku.edu/exhibits/show/naismith150/collections/radio-interview

Provided by Kansas University

University of Michigan

Circular to public educators, no date

Letters on basketball in Canada, 1930

Letter to Bruce Etchison, February 24, 1939

Letter to Robert H. Sturm, January 7, 1930

James Naismith Collection, Duane Norman Diedrich Collection, William L. Clements Library, University of Michigan

University of Nebraska

"The Origin of Basketball," *Basketball: Its Origin and Development*, 1941

Notes

Preface

1. Carlson, *Making March Madness*, 1.
2. Carlson, *Making March Madness*, 1.

Introduction

1. J. Naismith, *Basketball*, 33. Citations refer to the Association Press edition.
2. J. Naismith, *Basketball*, 33.
3. J. Naismith, *Basketball*, 33.
4. James Naismith, "Origin of Basket Ball" (presented at Forum, Springfield College, January 5, 1932).
5. J. Naismith, *Basketball*, 35.
6. J. Naismith, *Basketball*, 36.
7. J. Naismith, *Basketball*, 36.
8. J. Naismith, "Origin of Basket Ball."
9. Stuart Naismith with Douglas Stark, "Papa Jimmy: The Grandson of James Naismith Remembers the Game's Inventor as a Delightful and Sweet Man Who Loved to Laugh and Have Fun," *Hall of Fame Tip-Off Program* (Basketball Hall of Fame), November 22, 2000, 45.
10. J. Naismith, *Basketball*, 21
11. J. Naismith, *Basketball*, 23
12. S. Naismith and Stark, "Papa Jimmy," 45.
13. J. Naismith, *Basketball*, 23.
14. School for Christian Workers, Springfield, Mass.: Catalogs and Printed Materials, 1885–1890, Springfield College.
15. School for Christian Workers, Springfield, Mass.: Catalogs and Printed Materials, 1885–1890.
16. "Physical Education in the Young Men's Christian Association," Luther Gulick Papers, col. 14, box 5, folder 2, Springfield College, Springfield MA.
17. J. Naismith, *Basketball*, 38.
18. James Naismith, "Basketball—a Game the World Plays," *Rotarian*, January 1939.
19. J. Naismith, *Basketball*, 39.

20. J. Naismith, *Basketball*, 39.
21. J. Naismith, *Basketball*, 39.
22. J. Naismith, *Basketball*, 40.
23. J. Naismith, *Basketball*, 41.
24. J. Naismith, *Basketball*, 43.
25. J. Naismith, *Basketball*, 33.
26. J. Naismith, *Basketball*, 44.
27. J. Naismith, *Basketball*, 46.
28. J. Naismith, *Basketball*, 47.
29. J. Naismith, "Origin of Basket Ball."
30. J. Naismith, *Basketball*, 52–53.
31. J. Naismith, *Basketball*, 56.
32. J. Naismith, *Basketball*, 56.
33. Ernest Hildner interview, Naismith Memorial Basketball Hall of Fame, Springfield MA.
34. "Last of First Basketballers: Rap Freeze, Audiences, Amount of Whistle Tooting," *Philadelphia Inquirer*, December 26, n.d.
35. J. Naismith, "Basketball—a Game the World Plays."
36. "Basket Football Game," *Springfield Republican*, March 12, 1892, 6.
37. "Basket Football Game."
38. "A New Game of Ball," *New York Times*, April 26, 1892, 2.
39. "New Game of Ball."
40. Devaney, *The Story of Basketball*, 15.
41. Peterson, *Cages to Jump Shots*, 84.
42. "Dr. J. A. Naismith Is Dead in Kansas," *New York Times*, November 28, 1939, 25.
43. S. Naismith and Stark, "Papa Jimmy," 46.
44. "Dr. J. A. Naismith Is Dead in Kansas."
45. "Dr. J. A. Naismith Is Dead in Kansas."
46. "Dr. Naismith, Who Started Basketball in 1891, Dies," *Philadelphia Inquirer*, November 29, 1939, 30.
47. Rains, *James Naismith*, 88.
48. S. Naismith and Stark, "Papa Jimmy," 46.
49. Katz, *Breaking Through*, 12.

1. Origins, Growth, Development

1. Due to the difficulty in the original source of this document, an editorial decision was made to add brackets, which indicates that this is what we believe the original text to say.
2. Brackets here are original in the *McGill News* publication of the letter.
3. Brackets here are original in the *McGill News* publication of the letter.

HOW BASKETBALL STARTED

1. Due to the difficulty in the original source of this document, an editorial decision was made to add brackets, which indicates that this is what we believe the original text to say.

5. Correspondence

FORMAL CHALLENGES

1. Brackets here are original to the documentation provided by Springfield College.

Bibliography

Carlson, Chad. *Making March Madness: The Early Years of the* NCAA, NIT, *and College Basketball Championships, 1922–1951.* Fayetteville: University of Arkansas Press, 2017.

Devaney, John. *The Story of Basketball.* New York: Random House, 1976.

Dewar, John. "The Life and Professional Contributions of James Naismith." PhD diss., Florida State University, 1965.

Johnson, Scott Morrow. *Phog: The Most Influential Man in Basketball.* Lincoln: University of Nebraska Press, 2016.

Katz, Milton S. *Breaking Through: John B. McLendon, Basketball Legend and Civil Rights Pioneer.* Fayetteville: University of Arkansas Press, 2007.

Kerkhoff, Blair. *Phog Allen: The Father of Coaching Basketball.* Indianapolis IN: Masters Press, 1996.

Naismith, James. *Basketball: Its Origin and Development.* Lincoln: University of Nebraska Press, 1996.

———. *Basketball: Its Origin and Development.* New York: Association Press, 1941.

Peterson, Robert. *Cages to Jump Shots: Pro Basketball's Early Years.* New York: Oxford University Press, 1990.

Rains, Rob. *James Naismith: The Man Who Invented Basketball.* With Hellen Carpenter. Philadelphia: Temple University Press, 2009.

Webb, Bernice Larson. *The Basketball Man: James Naismith.* Lawrence KS: Kappelman's Historic Collections, 1994.

Wolff, Alexander, ed. *Basketball: Great Writings about America's Game.* With a foreword by Kareem Abdul-Jabbar. New York: Library of America, 2018.

Printed in the USA
CPSIA information can be obtained
at www.ICGtesting.com
LVHW05025408I223
766026LV00031B/408